Endangered, Threatened, and Depleted Marine Mammals in U.S. Waters

A Review of Species Classification Systems and Listed Species

Prepared for the Marine Mammal Commission by

Lloyd Lowry
David W. Laist
Elizabeth Taylor

2007

This is one of five reports prepared in response to a directive from Congress to the Marine Mammal Commission to assess the effectiveness of protection programs for the most endangered marine mammals in U.S. waters.

CONTENTS

EXECUTIVE SUMMARY

I.   INTRODUCTION

In its 2004 appropriations bill, Congress directed the Marine Mammal Commission to "review the biological viability of the most endangered marine mammal populations and make recommendations regarding the cost-effectiveness of current protection programs." This report identifies "the most endangered marine mammal populations" in U.S. waters, evaluates the criteria and methods used to place marine mammal species and populations on the major protected species lists, and reviews current data on their biological status.

II.   DESCRIPTION OF CLASSIFICATION SYSTEMS

Endangered Species Act

The Endangered Species Act (ESA), passed in 1973, employs a two-category system for listing species either as endangered ("in danger of extinction throughout all or a significant portion of its range") or threatened ("likely to become endangered in the foreseeable future"). Congress left the task of defining these terms to the federal agencies responsible for listing and delisting species, the Fish and Wildlife Service (FWS) and the National Marine Fisheries Service (NMFS). The ESA defines the term "species" to include "any subspecies of fish or wildlife or plants, and any distinct population segment of any species of vertebrate fish or wildlife which interbreeds when mature." Although the ESA is international in scope, different kinds of protection apply in U.S. and foreign territory and in federal jurisdiction versus state or private property.

The listing process begins with a review of the species' taxonomy, life history, habitat and ecological relationships, and population status, and an analysis of threats known or thought to be causing the species to be endangered or threatened. The threats analysis considers the following five factors for both listing and reclassification decisions:

- present or threatened destruction, modification, or curtailment of its habitat or range;
- overutilization for commercial, recreational, scientific, or educational purposes;
- disease or predation;
- inadequacy of existing regulatory mechanisms; and
- other natural or manmade factors affecting its continued existence.

In practice, the agencies often use what has been called a "weight of the evidence" approach in which all extinction risk factors for which information is available are considered in the analysis but without a strict formula for combining the appraisals of the respective factors.

Marine Mammal Protection Act

The Marine Mammal Protection Act (MMPA) uses population stocks (or simply stocks) as its unit of conservation and defines a stock as "a group of marine mammals of the same species or smaller taxa in a common spatial arrangement, that interbreed when mature." The MMPA provides general protection to all marine mammal stocks and additional protection to those designated as "depleted." A species or population stock is considered depleted if it is below its optimum sustainable population (OSP) or if it is listed under the ESA. The MMPA defines OSP as "the number of animals which will result in the maximum productivity of the population or the species, keeping in mind the carrying capacity of the habitat and the health of the ecosystem of which they form a constituent element." The responsible agencies have gone considerably farther in standardizing and quantifying criteria for evaluating status under the MMPA than they have for the ESA, and they have developed formulas relating to population size, carrying capacity, population growth rates, and incidental mortality rates. Similar to the ESA, the MMPA is international in scope but applies in different ways in U.S. and foreign territory.

IUCN–The World Conservation Union

IUCN–The World Conservation Union, through its Species Survival Commissions, evaluates the status of species, subspecies, and geographical populations worldwide and produces its "Red List" of threatened species. Its rule-based classification system uses both quantitative and qualitative criteria to place species within categories depending on the predicted degree of extinction risk. The criteria include measures of current population size, trend in population size, population structure, size of occupied range, and quantitative analysis of probability of extinction. The criteria can be applied to any taxonomic unit at or below the species level. Although the categories and criteria are intended primarily for global taxon assessments, they also may be applied at regional, national, or local levels. The IUCN assessments are not directly comparable with ESA listings, in part because they are not always done for the same taxonomic unit, and in part because the IUCN categories do not automatically carry a regulatory consequence so the terms like "endangered" are not fully portable between the classification systems. However, all 22 marine mammal taxa listed under the ESA and MMPA are considered in one way or another by the IUCN.

Summary of Current Listing Status

Out of the 22 marine mammal taxa reviewed, the ESA lists 14 as endangered and 4 as threatened; 4 are not listed. The MMPA lists all 22 taxa as depleted. The IUCN lists 1 of the taxa as extinct, 1 as critically endangered, 10 as endangered, 6 as vulnerable, 3 as lower risk, and 1 as data deficient (see Table 2). Both populations of sirenians are listed as endangered under the ESA and vulnerable on the IUCN Red List. Both populations of sea otters are listed as threatened under the ESA and endangered on the IUCN Red List. For the pinnipeds, three populations are listed under the ESA as endangered and two as threatened; one is not listed. The IUCN lists one pinniped population as extinct, three as endangered, and two as vulnerable. For the cetaceans, nine populations are listed as endangered and three are not listed under the ESA. The IUCN lists one cetacean population as critically endangered, five as endangered, two as vulnerable, three as lower risk, and one as data deficient.

Current IUCN, ESA, and MMPA approaches differ with respect to listing units. IUCN listings are often applied to entire species worldwide, while recent ESA and MMPA listings have been based on population segments or stocks. Under the ESA, all eight species of large whales are considered on a worldwide basis because they were first listed under the 1969 Endangered Species Conservation Act, a precursor to the ESA. Of the taxa considered here, the IUCN lists 10 species on a worldwide basis, including 5 species of large whales. Although many of the species considered include multiple isolated or relatively discrete population units, the nature of those units is often either not described or not yet recognized in the evaluation/listing process. More recent listings by stocks and population segments indicate that this is an evolving process.

In the United States, 11 marine mammal taxa were listed after passage of the Endangered Species Preservation Act or the Endangered Species Conservation Act, and none was subject to a baseline assessment of the five listing factors detailing the rationale for listing. Seven taxa were listed subsequent to passage of the ESA, one taxon was evaluated for listing and rejected, and three have not been evaluated. Under the MMPA, 16 taxa are listed as depleted due to their ESA listing, 5 taxa were listed following an OSP evaluation, and 1 taxon was listed without an OSP evaluation.

Available Data and Current Biological Status

A review of the data currently available on various biological attributes of listed species indicates that the quality of the data varies greatly. For only five taxa was data availability ranked as good in four or more of the six data categories considered. However, if both good and fair data quality are considered, 11 taxa have good or fair data in all six categories and 2 have good or fair in five categories. At the other extreme, 4 taxa have poor data availability in all of the categories and 8 in three or more categories. For taxa with good-to-fair abundance estimates, population sizes range from 8 for AT1 killer whales to 688,028 for eastern North Pacific fur seals. The taxa with the smallest estimated abundances are AT1 killer whales (8), North Pacific right whales (minimum 23), southern resident killer whales (84), Cook Inlet beluga whales (278), and Hawaiian monk seals (1,252). AT1 killer whales and Cook Inlet beluga whales are not listed under the ESA.

Major Findings and Conclusions

In many cases the ESA, MMPA, and IUCN listings have not kept pace with the growing body of knowledge on population (or stock) structure, although the more recent listing actions have considered biologically reasonable population units. In particular, the ESA lists all species of large whales as endangered on a worldwide basis despite the fact that many are known to exist in discrete regional populations. For large whales listed under the ESA, NMFS should (1) identify distinct population segments based on recent information on population structure and (2) evaluate the listing status of each newly identified population segment.

Some other taxa currently listed under the ESA should be reevaluated and possibly reclassified. For instance, Caribbean monk seals might be declared extinct, eastern Steller sea lions might be delisted, western Steller sea lions might be downlisted, and Cook Inlet beluga whales and AT1 killer whales might be listed as endangered or threatened.

There is concern among scientists that a lack of data has precluded the listing of some taxa that may in fact be endangered, threatened, or depleted (e.g., beaked whales). For those taxa, scientists often do not know what the population units are that should be of conservation concern, what their historical and current abundances were and are, whether numbers are currently increasing or decreasing, and what factors may be threatening the population. Without such data, it is essentially impossible to conduct thorough status reviews or to compare population status with the listing criteria used by any system. A more robust decision system is needed for coping with the likelihood that some species for which there is little available data are nevertheless endangered and in need of conservation attention.

I. INTRODUCTION

In fiscal year 2004 the Congress directed the Marine Mammal Commission to "review the biological viability of the most endangered marine mammal populations and make recommendations regarding the cost-effectiveness of current protection programs." The Commission interpreted, and confirmed with staff of the Senate Appropriations Committee, that this directive was focused on marine mammals occurring substantially in U.S. waters of the Atlantic, Pacific, and Arctic Oceans. The Commission undertook a series of reviews and prepared two reports (including this one) to provide a basis for its response to Congress. The purpose of this report is to summarize relevant information on the status of marine mammal species and populations that have been formally identified as requiring special protection. The second report (Weber and Laist 2007) reviews existing protection programs for the listed species. The other related reviews undertaken as part of the Commission's response to the directive have (1) examined modeling efforts to predict marine mammal population trends and assess their utility for evaluating degree of endangerment, and (2) assessed the cost-effectiveness of the recovery program for North Atlantic right whales.

The first line of protection for marine mammals in U.S. waters results from actions prescribed by the Endangered Species Act (ESA) and the Marine Mammal Protection Act (MMPA). Both Acts establish provisions for listing marine mammal species and populations with special conservation needs. The ESA creates a two-tiered system under which species and populations may be listed as "endangered" or "threatened." The MMPA establishes a single category system for listing species or populations as "depleted." Once listed, a species or population is eligible for additional protection measures specified in the Acts. At the time this report was drafted, 20 marine mammal species or populations occurring regularly in U.S. waters were listed under one or both Acts. Taxonomic revisions accepted since ESA listings were made have recognized northern right whales as two separate species (i.e., North Atlantic and North Pacific right whales) and West Indian manatees as consisting of two subspecies (i.e., Florida manatees and Antillean manatees). For this review, we considered each of these species and subspecies separately, thereby increasing the number of taxa considered from 20 to 22. Although marine mammals also are "listed" under many other classification systems of various organizations, the most widely recognized international system is the Red List of Threatened Species prepared by the International Union for the Conservation of Nature–The World Conservation Union (IUCN). Begun in the 1960s, the IUCN Red List has evolved into a multi-tiered classification system developed to identify species in greatest need of protection on a global basis.

To identify which marine mammals in U.S. waters are most endangered, this report reviews the ESA, MMPA, and IUCN species classification systems and summarizes information on the listing status and biological status of those species and populations now included under them. For each of the three classification systems, the report describes the criteria and process for listing species. For the listed species and populations, it summarizes available information on distribution and identified conservation units, evaluation and listing history, major biological datasets, and current biological status and trend. Based on this information, summary tables are provided to compare information across taxa. The findings and conclusions in this report are those of the authors and do not necessarily reflect those of the Marine Mammal Commission. They are intended to provide background information and suggestions for consideration by the Commission in developing its report to Congress.

II. MAJOR LISTING SYSTEMS FOR SPECIES AND POPULATIONS AT RISK

Endangered Species Act

Protection for endangered species under U.S. federal law began with the Endangered Species Preservation Act (ESPA) of 1966 (Public Law 89-669). This legislation directed the Secretary of the Interior to carry out conservation programs for endangered species and authorized measures to protect habitats. Species were to be determined as threatened with extinction upon a finding by the Secretary "after consultation with the affected States, that its existence is endangered because its habitat is threatened with destruction, drastic modification, or severe curtailment, or because of overexploitation, disease, predation, or because of other factors, and that its survival requires assistance." The Secretary was directed to seek the advice and recommendations of interested persons, including wildlife scientists, and to publish in the *Federal Register* the names of all species found to be threatened with extinction.

The ESPA was followed by the Endangered Species Conservation Act (ESCA) of 1969 (Public Law 91-135). This legislation authorized the Secretary to promulgate a list of wildlife threatened with extinction worldwide and to prohibit their importation into the United States. It also required that listing of endangered species be done pursuant to the rulemaking procedures of the Administrative Procedure Act.

The ESPA and the ESCA were superseded by the Endangered Species Act (ESA) of 1973 (Public Law 93-205), which was subsequently amended substantially in 1978, 1982, 1984, and 1988. With each succeeding Act, the list of already listed species was largely carried forward, notwithstanding changes in definitions and listing procedures. The purposes and policies of the current ESA as amended are stated in section 2 of the Act:

> (b) PURPOSES.—The purposes of this Act are to provide a means whereby the ecosystems upon which endangered species and threatened species depend may be conserved, to provide a program for the conservation of such endangered species and threatened species, and to take such steps as may be appropriate to achieve the purposes of the treaties and conventions set forth in subsection (a) of this section.
> (c) POLICY.—(1) It is further declared to be the policy of Congress that all Federal departments and agencies shall seek to conserve endangered species and threatened species and shall utilize their authorities in furtherance of the purposes of this Act.
> (2) It is further declared to be the policy of Congress that Federal agencies shall cooperate with State and local agencies to resolve water resource issues in concert with conservation of endangered species.

The ESA employs a two-category system for listing species either as endangered ("in danger of extinction throughout all or a significant portion of its range"; sec. 3[6]) or threatened ("likely to become endangered in the foreseeable future"; sec. 3[20]). An implicit third category is "not threatened or endangered," which includes species that have been evaluated but not listed as well as those that have never been evaluated. Congress left the task of defining these and other terms in the statute to the two federal agencies responsible for listing and delisting species, the Fish and Wildlife Service (FWS) and the National Marine Fisheries Service (NMFS). In 1984 NMFS and FWS published joint regulations to govern the ESA listing process and the designation of critical habitat (50 C.F.R. §424). However, a multi-agency working group charged with making recommendations on the use of quantitative criteria concluded that the guidelines developed by those agencies have not yet achieved the desired level of consistency, standardization, and objectivity in the decision process for listing, reclassifying, or delisting species (DeMaster et al. 2004). The Act requires that recovery plans for endangered species include "objective, measurable criteria which, when met, would result in a determination, in accordance with the provisions of this section, that the species be removed from the list" (sec. 4(f)(1)(B)[ii]). This suggests that Congress intended that specific criteria be used in listing decisions. Recently NMFS has published reports recommending criteria to use for evaluating ESA listing status of marine species in general (DeMaster et al. 2004) and large whales in particular (Angliss et al. 2002).

The ESA defines the term "species" to include "any subspecies of fish or wildlife or plants, and any distinct population segment of any species of vertebrate fish or wildlife which interbreeds when mature" (sec. 3[16]). FWS and NMFS agreed on a joint policy for identifying "distinct population segments" (DPSs) in 1996 (61 Fed. Reg. 4722). The policy states that DPSs are to be determined based on three sequential considerations: (1) the discreteness of the population relative to the rest of the species; (2) the significance of the population segment to the species; and (3) the population segment's conservation status in relation to the ESA's standards for listing (i.e., is the population segment endangered or threatened when treated as if it were a species?).

The policy goes on to state: "Listing, delisting, or reclassifying distinct vertebrate population segments may allow the Services to protect and conserve species and the ecosystems upon which they depend before large-scale decline occurs that would necessitate listing a species or subspecies throughout its entire range. This may allow protection and recovery of declining organisms in a more timely and less costly manner, and on a smaller scale than the more costly and extensive efforts that might be needed to recover an entire species or subspecies."

The listing process begins with a review of the species' taxonomy, life history, habitat and ecological relationships, and population status, and an analysis of threats that may be causing it to be endangered or threatened. The threats analysis must, at a minimum, consider the following five factors specified in section 4(a)(1) of the Act:

- present or threatened destruction, modification, or curtailment of its habitat or range;
- overutilization for commercial, recreational, scientific, or educational purposes;
- disease or predation;
- inadequacy of existing regulatory mechanisms; and
- other natural or manmade factors affecting its continued existence.

These factors serve as a checklist to be used in evaluating species status and indicate that any threat including "natural" sources can cause a species to be at risk and to merit ESA protection. In practice, the agencies often use what has been called a "weight of the evidence" approach in which all extinction risk factors for which information is available are considered in the analysis but without a strict formula for combining the appraisals of the respective factors (DeMaster et al. 2004). The ESA requires that listing decisions be based solely on the best scientific and commercial data available (sec. 4[b][1][A]), and it prohibits the consideration of economic impacts in making species listing decisions. The Act also requires FWS and NMFS to "conduct, at least once every five years, a review of all species included in a list" and "determine on the basis of such review whether any such species should—(i) be removed from such list; (ii) be changed in status from an endangered species to a threatened species; or (iii) be changed in status from a threatened species to an endangered species" (sec. 4[c][2]). Since 1994 FWS and NMFS have had a formal policy that listing recommendations and recovery plans are subject to independent peer review (59 Fed. Reg. 34270).

Marine Mammal Protection Act

The Marine Mammal Protection Act (MMPA; Public Law 92-522) was passed in 1972 and has been amended several times, most recently in 2003. The first two findings in the Act pertain to protection for endangered species, and state (sec. 2):

> (1) certain species and population stocks of marine mammals are, or may be, in danger of extinction or depletion as a result of man's activities;
> (2) such species and population stocks should not be permitted to diminish beyond the point at which they cease to be a significant functioning element in the ecosystem of which they are a part, and, consistent with this major objective, they should not be permitted to diminish below their optimum sustainable population. Further measures should be immediately taken to replenish any species or population stock which has already diminished below that population. In particular, efforts should be made to protect essential habitats, including the rookeries, mating grounds, and areas of similar significance for each species of marine mammal from the adverse effect of man's actions.

The MMPA provides general protection to all marine mammal species and population stocks and provides additional protections to those designated as "depleted." Section 3(1) defines the term "depleted" as any case in which:

> (A) the Secretary, after consultation with the Marine Mammal Commission and the Committee of Scientific Advisors on Marine Mammals established under title II of this Act, determines that a species or population stock is below its optimum sustainable population;

(B) a State, to which authority for the conservation and management of a species or population stock is transferred under section 109, determines that such species or stock is below its optimum sustainable population; or

(C) a species or population stock is listed as an endangered species or a threatened species under the Endangered Species Act of 1973.

Section 3(11) defines the term "population stock" or "stock" as "a group of marine mammals of the same species or smaller taxa in a common spatial arrangement, that interbreed when mature."

A species or stock that is not listed under the ESA will be classified as depleted only if it is determined to be below its optimum sustainable population (OSP) level. Section 3(9) of the MMPA defines OSP as "…with respect to any population stock, the number of animals which will result in the maximum productivity of the population or the species, keeping in mind the carrying capacity of the habitat and the health of the ecosystem of which they form a constituent element."

NMFS regulations (50 C.F.R. § 216.3) clarify the definition of OSP as a population size that falls within a range from the largest supportable within the ecosystem (i.e., carrying capacity or K) to its maximum net productivity level (MNPL). Maximum net productivity is the greatest net annual increment in population numbers or biomass resulting from additions to the population from reproduction, less losses due to natural mortality. Historically, MNPL has been expressed as a range of values (generally 50 to 70 percent of K) determined theoretically by estimating what size stock in relation to the original stock size will produce the maximum net increase in population (42 Fed. Reg. 12010). The midpoint of this range (60 percent) was used to determine whether dolphin stocks in the eastern tropical Pacific Ocean were depleted (42 Fed. Reg. 64548) and in the final rule governing the taking of marine mammals incidental to commercial fishing operations (45 Fed. Reg. 72178).

Section 115 of the MMPA describes procedures for reviewing the status of species. It specifies that, when designation of a species as depleted may be appropriate, "the Secretary shall only make such a determination by issuance of a rule, after notice and opportunity for public comment and after a call for information" that should be made available in a status review. It also states that any determination made shall be based "solely on the basis of the best scientific information available." There is no required schedule for reexamining the status of depleted species once listed.

IUCN–The World Conservation Union

The Species Survival Commission (SSC) of the IUCN evaluates the status of species worldwide and produces its "Red List of Threatened Species" (see http://www.redlist.org). To encourage consistency in classifications within broad taxon groups, "Red List Authorities" are established for all taxonomic groups included on the List. In most cases, the Red List Authority is the SSC Specialist Group responsible for the species, group of species, or specific geographic area. The Red List Authorities are charged with ensuring that all species within their jurisdiction are evaluated against the Red List categories at least once every ten years and, if possible, every five years. The minimum documentation required for an assessment is specified, and assessments are reviewed both within the Red List Authority and by outside peer reviewers. Once approved, a classification is added, or a change is made, to the Red List.

IUCN uses a rule-based classification system with both quantitative and qualitative criteria to place species at risk in eight categories (IUCN 2001; Table 1). Those categories include "data deficient" as well as a distinction between "extinct" and "extinct in the wild." The criteria are based on current population size (expressed as mature individuals), trends in population size (past, present, and projected), population structure, size and degree of fragmentation of range (in two senses: extent of occurrence and area of occupancy), and quantitative analysis of probability of extinction (see Appendix 1).

The IUCN criteria are designed for application to any taxonomic unit at or below the species level and are the same for all taxa. Although the categories and criteria are intended primarily for global taxon assessments, they also may be applied at regional, national, or local levels. When applied at a more restricted level, a taxon may merit a different category than it does in a global assessment.

III. STATUS OF LISTED MARINE MAMMALS

West Indian manatee, Florida subspecies (*Trichechus manatus latirostris*) (ESA – endangered[1]; IUCN – vulnerable; MMPA – depleted)

<u>Distribution and conservation units</u>

The Florida manatee is one of two recognized subspecies of the West Indian (also called Caribbean) manatee (Rice 1998). Except for a few summer migrants that have traveled as far north as Rhode Island and as far west as Texas, Florida manatees occur only in waters of the southeastern United States. In winter they are limited almost exclusively to Florida. Four subpopulations are identified in the Florida Manatee Recovery Plan (FWS 2001): two on the eastern coast of Florida (one in the upper St. Johns River and the other along the Atlantic coast) and two on the western coast (one in southwest Florida from Tampa Bay south and the other in northwest Florida north of Tampa Bay). These four subpopulations were identified for management purposes and are not considered distinct population segments for purposes of listing under the ESA.

<u>History of evaluation and listing</u>

The Florida manatee is under the jurisdiction of FWS. Milestones relative to the subspecies' listing include the following:

- Subspecies listed as endangered under the ESPA in 1967.
- Entire species listed as endangered under the ESCA in 1970.
- Endangered status carried forward under the ESA in 1973.
- Qualified as depleted under the MMPA in 1973 by virtue of its listing under the ESA.
- West Indian manatee recovery plan first adopted in 1980.
- First revision of recovery plan specific to the Florida population adopted in 1989.
- Second revision of Florida manatee recovery plan adopted in 1996.
- Subspecies listed as vulnerable by the IUCN in 1996.
- Third revision of Florida manatee recovery plan adopted in 2001.
- Species status currently being reviewed by IUCN.
- Species status under the ESA currently being reexamined by FWS.

No detailed explanation was given when the Florida subspecies of the West Indian manatee was listed as endangered under the ESPA in 1967 (32 Fed. Reg. 4001). Based on correspondence in FWS files, it apparently was listed at the recommendation of the State of Florida because of habitat concerns related to coastal development and boating activity. The entire species was later included on the list of endangered species in the 1970 ESCA (35 Fed. Reg. 18319) and the 1973 ESA.

---

[1] West Indian manatees are currently listed under the ESA as a single species; however, taxonomic studies (Domning and Hayek 1986) recognize two subspecies, one in Florida and the other from Central America to Brazil, including the Antilles.

Because the species was already listed when the ESA was passed, a formal analysis of threats and ESA listing factors was not done at that time.

The 2001 Florida Manatee Recovery Plan states its goal as "to assure the long-term viability of the Florida manatee in the wild, allowing initially for reclassification from endangered to threatened status (downlisting) and ultimately removal from the List of Endangered and Threatened Wildlife (delisting)" (FWS 2001). The plan provides criteria for downlisting and delisting the population based on "implementing, monitoring and addressing the effectiveness of conservation measures to reduce or remove threats which will lead to a healthy and self-sustaining population" (FWS 2001). The criteria are based largely on protecting important habitats (warm-water refuges, migratory corridors, feeding areas, calving and nursing areas) and controlling sources of human-caused mortality (boat strikes, entrapment in water control structures, fishing gear entanglement). Criteria also specify demographic benchmarks for survival, reproduction, and population growth rate. Downlisting and delisting decisions require that each of the four identified subpopulations meet the demographic benchmarks.

Major threats identified in the 2001 recovery plan were human-caused mortality (principally from boat strikes and to a lesser extent entrapment in flood gates and navigation locks), decreasing availability of warm-water refuges, and coastal development (FWS 2001). The recovery plan recommended that a full ESA status review be initiated in 2003. In April 2005 FWS announced its intention to conduct a status review and requested interested parties to submit relevant information (70 Fed. Reg. 19780).

In its 1996 Red List, the IUCN SSC listed the Florida manatee as vulnerable based on criterion A2d (IUCN 1996). The status of the taxon was evaluated most recently by the IUCN Sirenian Specialist Group at the International Mammalogical Congress in August 2005. The Group concluded that the Florida manatee should be listed as endangered based on criteria A3c, A3d, and C1 (Taylor et al. 2006), but such a change has not yet been made to the Red List. Potential threats that were identified at the time were watercraft mortality and serious injury, red tides, loss of warm-water habitat, habitat loss in general, disease, and possibly contaminants (J. Reynolds, pers. comm.).

Florida manatees are considered depleted under the MMPA because of their ESA listing. Their status relative to OSP has not been evaluated.

Available data

Few directed studies were conducted on manatees in Florida prior to listing under the ESPA in 1967. Currently, however, they are among the most extensively studied marine mammals in the United States. Dedicated research since the late 1970s has produced several important long-term datasets. Most research is funded by federal and state agencies and carried out by scientists with the Department of the Interior (initially FWS and now the U.S. Geological Survey) and the State of Florida (the Fish and Wildlife Research Institute in the Florida Fish and Wildlife Conservation

Commission). Cooperating scientists with aquariums, universities, and other research institutes also contribute significant amounts of information.

The most extensive datasets are (1) manatee mortality records including (where possible) age estimates, causes of death, and archived tissue samples for more than 5,000 animals since the late 1970s; (2) a photo-identification catalogue with associated life history data including information on reproduction and survival rates for more than 2,000 animals; (3) aerial surveys and counts of animals at major winter refuges (several dating back to the late 1970s or early 1980s); and (4) satellite tracking data for a large number of individuals in many parts of the state. Many of these data have been compiled in a GIS system developed and maintained by the Fish and Wildlife Research Institute. Information also is available on manatee foraging behavior in numerous locations. Data also are collected on vessel traffic in manatee habitat to assess efforts to reduce collisions with boats and evaluate the efficacy of existing regulations.

Several population models have been developed for Florida manatees including a stage-based population viability analysis (PVA) model (Runge et al. 2004).

Current biological status

Surveys in the late 1970s indicated at least 800 to 1,000 manatees in Florida at that time (FWS 1980). The minimum population size for Florida manatees is now estimated at 3,300 animals based on aerial and ground counts in 2001 (Haubold et al. 2005). Most manatee biologists believe that abundance has increased since the early 1980s although improvements in survey methods probably account for at least some of the differences in estimates between then and now. The Manatee Recovery Team, with advice from its Population Status Working Group, evaluates status separately for each region using available data on reproduction, survival, and population growth. Based on that evaluation, the Northwest and Upper St. Johns River subpopulations appear to be increasing steadily, the Atlantic subpopulation appears to be demographically stable but evidence regarding its recent growth rate is inconclusive, and data for the Southwest subpopulation are not sufficient to evaluate status. The two subpopulations of uncertain status comprise more than 80 percent of the total population. Several of the human-related causes of mortality discussed above are likely responsible for limiting population growth.

FWS published the most recent stock assessment report (SAR) for the Florida stock of West Indian manatees in 2000 (see http://www.nmfs.noaa.gov/pr/sars/species.htm). The SAR presents outdated information on population size and trend. It calculates a PBR of 3.0 and notes that the level of human-related mortality (primarily from watercraft collisions and water control structures) greatly exceeds the PBR.

West Indian manatee, Antillean subspecies (*Trichechus manatus manatus*), Puerto Rican population (ESA – endangered[2]; IUCN – vulnerable; MMPA – depleted)

Distribution and conservation units

The Antillean manatee is one of two recognized subspecies of the West Indian (also called Caribbean) manatee (Rice 1998). The largest known groups of Antillean manatees occupy waters of Belize and southeastern Mexico. They are also fairly numerous (but poorly surveyed) around certain rivers in Colombia and Brazil. However, distribution is very patchy due to past hunting and discontinuous habitat (Lefebvre et al. 1989). In many countries, manatees are now very rare or absent altogether. With regard to waters under U.S. jurisdiction, manatees occur in Puerto Rico where they are most abundant along the southern and eastern coasts. They generally do not occur in the Virgin Islands (FWS 1986).

History of evaluation and listing

The Antillean manatee is under the jurisdiction of FWS. Milestones relative to the population's listing include the following:

- Entire species listed as endangered under the ESCA in 1970.
- Endangered status carried forward under the ESA in 1973.
- Qualified as depleted under the MMPA in 1973 by virtue of its listing under the ESA.
- West Indian manatee recovery plan (including Puerto Rico) first adopted in 1980.
- Puerto Rico manatee recovery plan adopted in 1986.
- Listed as vulnerable by the IUCN in 1996.
- Status being reviewed by IUCN in 2005.

The ESPA in 1967 listed the Florida subspecies of West Indian manatee as endangered but did not list the Antillean subspecies (32 Fed. Reg. 4001). When the ESCA was passed in 1970, the list of endangered species included the entire West Indian manatee species (35 Fed. Reg. 18319). No detailed explanation was given for the ESCA listing. The situation remained the same with passage of the ESA in 1973, and because the species was already listed when the Act was passed, a formal analysis of threats and ESA listing factors was not done at that time.

The Recovery Plan for the Puerto Rico Population of the West Indian Manatee states its goal as "to recover the population of manatees in Puerto Rico so that the Puerto Rican population of the Antillean manatee (*T. m. manatus*) can be delisted" (FWS 1986). The recovery plan does not specify criteria for downlisting and delisting because data on historical and current abundance are lacking. The plan identifies entanglement in gillnets and industrial development as factors that could be affecting the population and states that there is no evidence that natural factors are causing excessive mortality.

---

[2] See note 1 above.

In its 1996 Red List, IUCN listed the Antillean manatee as vulnerable based on criteria A1c, A1d, and C2a (IUCN 1996). The status of the taxon was most recently evaluated by the IUCN Sirenian Specialist Group at the International Mammalogical Congress in August 2005. The Group concluded that the Antillean manatee should be listed as endangered based on criteria A4c, A4d, and C1 (Taylor et al. 2006), but such a change has not yet been made to the Red List. Potential threats that were identified in the evaluation were habitat degradation and loss, hunting, accidental mortality, pollution, and human disturbance. Conservation actions are complicated by the fact that the subspecies occupies waters of a number of countries.

Antillean manatees are considered depleted under the MMPA because of their ESA listing. Their status relative to OSP has not been evaluated.

Available data

Other than passing historical references to manatees in Puerto Rico, there is virtually no information on this population prior to its listing under the ESCA in 1967. Since then, information has improved significantly but remains very limited. Most research has been funded by the Department of the Interior and the U.S. Navy and is carried out by scientists with the U.S. Geological Survey and non-governmental institutions. Available data sources include counts from sporadic island-wide aerial surveys done since 1978, mortality records from carcass salvage efforts, several satellite tracking studies, and sighting records for few photo-identified individuals. Substantive long-term datasets are not available. Data on manatees in the Virgin Islands are limited to opportunistic sighting reports.

No models designed specifically for population viability analysis have been developed for the Antillean manatee population.

Current biological status

The abundance of Antillean manatees is largely unknown. FWS published a SAR for the Puerto Rico portion of the stock in 1995 (see http://www.nmfs.noaa.gov/pr/sars/species.htm), which cites a 1994 survey that produced a count of 86 manatees. The SAR uses that number as a minimum population estimate and calculates a PBR of 0. It states that Antillean manatees are a strategic stock because of high levels of human-caused mortality relative to population size and severe threats to important habitats. There are no good data to assess population trend in Puerto Rico, but overall the Antillean subspecies appears to be declining (J. Reynolds, pers. comm.).

Southern sea otter (*Enhydra lutris nereis*) (ESA – threatened; IUCN – endangered; MMPA – depleted)

Distribution and conservation units

Sea otters once occupied coastal waters all along the North Pacific rim from central Baja California to northern Japan, but their distribution is now discontinuous. Three subspecies are recognized in eastern Russia, Alaska-British Columbia-Washington, and California (Rice 1998). The southern (California) subspecies is geographically isolated from animals living farther north and differs from the other subspecies in cranial morphology (Wilson et al. 1991) and DNA characteristics (Cronin et al. 1996). The range currently occupied by the southern subspecies includes nearshore waters in central California from approximately Half Moon Bay to Point Conception. Also, a translocation program has established a small group of animals at San Nicolas Island.

History of evaluation and listing

The southern sea otter is under the jurisdiction of FWS. Milestones relative to the subspecies' listing include the following:

- Subspecies listed as threatened under the ESA in 1977.
- Qualified as depleted under the MMPA in 1977 by virtue of its listing under the ESA.
- First recovery plan adopted in 1982.
- Experimental population at San Nicolas Island established by translocation in 1987.
- Entire species listed as endangered by the IUCN in 2000.
- Revised recovery plan adopted in 2003.

In 1977 FWS determined that the southern sea otter was not endangered but should be listed as threatened under the ESA (42 Fed. Reg. 2965). The listing notice included an analysis of the five ESA listing factors that concluded as follows:

    A. *The present or threatened destruction, modification, or curtailment of its habitat or range*—The current range is much reduced from what it was in historical time, and that habitat is potentially jeopardized by oil spills, pollution, and competition with humans.

    B. *Overutilization for commercial, recreational, scientific, or educational purposes*—The original decline was caused largely by commercial exploitation. At the time of listing, illegal killing was known to occur but was not judged to be a current threat to the overall population.

    C. *Disease or predation*—These factors were not known to pose a serious threat at the time.

    D. *The inadequacy of existing regulatory mechanisms*—Existing laws were judged adequate to protect sea otters from direct taking, but methods for habitat protection were judged to be inadequate and would be improved with ESA listing.

    E. *Other natural or manmade factors affecting its continued existence*—The most serious potential threat was judged to be a large oil spill that could affect a large portion of the remaining population.

The 2003 recovery plan reiterates those threats and notes that pollution and incidental take in fisheries are recognized problems (FWS 2003). Other threats that have been identified include disease, shark predation, and illegal shooting (MMC 2004).

The goal stated in the 2003 recovery plan is "to establish the long-term viability of the southern sea otter population sufficiently to allow delisting of the species" (FWS 2003). The plan establishes the following quantitative criteria for reclassification and delisting based on spring survey counts using standardized methods:

- Reclassification as endangered should be considered if the average population size over a three-year period is less than or equal to 1,850.
- Sea otters should remain classified as threatened as long as the average population size over a three-year period is more than 1,850 and less than 3,090.
- Delisting should be considered when the average population size over a three-year period is more that 3,090.

The recovery plan also states that if the proposed criterion for delisting is reached, it will be necessary to do a full evaluation of the ESA's five listing factors prior to changing the listing status. Rationales for the development of the delisting criteria are described in Ralls et al. (1996).

The status of sea otters was evaluated by the IUCN Otter Specialist Group in 2000, and the species was listed by the IUCN as endangered based on criteria A1a, A1c, and A1e (IUCN 1996). The southern subspecies was not evaluated as a separate taxon. Threats identified at the time were oil pollution, killer whale predation, poaching, and fishery interactions.

Southern sea otters are considered as depleted under the MMPA because of their ESA listing. Their status relative to OSP has not been evaluated. However, FWS has estimated the lower bound of OSP at 8,400 animals for the entire California coast (FWS 2003). Because the lower bound of OSP is considerably greater than the population size at which southern sea otters would be considered for delisting under the ESA, it is possible that upon delisting the population would still be considered depleted under the MMPA.

Available data

Before listing under the ESA in 1977, information on southern sea otters was almost entirely limited to historical accounts of the fur trade and sporadic surveys done by the California Department of Fish and Game (CDFG) since the 1930s. Since 1977 a dedicated ongoing research program has developed involving the CDFG and the Department of the Interior, with significant contributions from the academic community and aquariums. The core of the research program has been standardized range-wide counts conducted annually in the spring and fall since 1982. The counts include information on the numbers of pups and independent animals. Data also have been collected on causes of and trends in mortality and on movement patterns. The former are from opportunistic and directed carcass salvage efforts; the latter are from radio tracking studies. Prey preferences, foraging patterns, and the effects of foraging otters on coastal marine communities also have been the subjects of focused research.

A population model has been developed for southern sea otters (T. Tinker and D. Doak, unpub.), but it has not been used for population viability analysis.

Current biological status

Estimates of the historical population of southern sea otters and estimates of carrying capacity for California are in general agreement at approximately 16,000 animals (Laidre et. al. 2001). By the early 1900s the southern sea otter was nearly extinct due to exploitation by fur hunters. A remnant group of perhaps 50 animals remained in central California when hunting was prohibited in 1911 under the North Pacific Fur Seal Convention. The number of sea otters generally increased along with the expansion of occupied range, and the population was estimated to number 1,789 in 1976, the year before ESA listing. The estimated population size was lower in 1983 (1,277) when annual spring counts using standardized methods began, but counts increased steadily to a peak in 1994 (2,359) and 1995 (2,377) before declining for several years. The population appears to have been increasing since about 2000, with the 2003 (2,505) and 2004 counts (2,825) the highest on record (see http://www.werc.usgs.gov/otters/ca-surveydata.html). In 2005 the count dropped slightly to 2,735.

FWS published the most recent SAR for southern sea otters in 1995 (see http://www.nmfs.noaa.gov/pr/sars/species.htm). The SAR provides outdated information on population size and trend. It notes that the population is classified as threatened and depleted and calculates a PBR of seven animals. However, this evaluation has no legal implications because southern sea otters are specifically exempted from the incidental take management process specified in section 118 of the MMPA.

Some translocated populations of northern sea otters have shown population growth of 17 to 20 percent per year (Estes 1990). However, in California overall population growth has been much slower, apparently due to elevated mortality rates that have caused periods of population decline. Potential causes for elevated mortality have been identified as increased rate of disease, entanglement in coastal fishing gear, and decreased abundance of food (FWS 2003).

Northern sea otter, southwest Alaska population (*Enhydra lutris kenyoni*) (ESA – threatened; IUCN – endangered; MMPA – depleted)

Distribution and conservation units

Sea otters once occupied coastal waters all around the North Pacific rim from central Baja California to northern Japan, but their distribution is now discontinuous. Sea otters in eastern Russia, Alaska-British Columbia-Washington (called northern), and California are recognized as separate subspecies (Rice 1998). The southwest Alaska population is a part of the northern subspecies that occurs along the Alaska Peninsula and in the Aleutian Islands and eastern Bering Sea. The range of the southwest Alaska population extends from the western Aleutian Islands at the U.S.-Russia border to Cook Inlet. It is considered a taxon distinct from those to the west and east because of geographical barriers and morphological and genetic differences (Gorbics and Bodkin 2001).

History of evaluation and listing

The northern sea otter is under the jurisdiction of FWS. Milestones relative to the population's listing include the following:

- Population added to the list of candidate species for ESA listing in 2000.
- Petitioned to list sea otters in the Aleutian Islands as endangered or threatened under the ESA in 2000, but no action taken.
- Entire species listed as endangered by IUCN in 2000.
- Denied petition to list "Alaska stock" of sea otters as depleted under the MMPA in 2001.
- Southwest Alaska distinct population segment listed as threatened under the ESA in 2005.

The 2005 ESA listing notice for the southwest Alaska distinct population segment (70 Fed. Reg. 46366) included an analysis of the five ESA listing factors that concluded as follows:

A. *The present or threatened destruction, modification, or curtailment of its habitat or range*—This factor is not known to have been important in the decline.
B. *Overutilization for commercial, recreational, scientific, or educational purposes*—There is no commercial use of sea otters, and subsistence harvests are relatively low and do not pose an immediate threat.
C. *Disease or predation*—There is no evidence that disease has caused the population decline. Predation by killer whales has been identified as the most likely cause of the decline.
D. *The inadequacy of existing regulatory mechanisms*—Provisions of the MMPA allow for regulation of subsistence take by Alaska Natives and incidental take by commercial fisheries. Because those factors do not appear to be what is threatening the population, the MMPA was judged inadequate to prevent the continuing decline.
E. *Other natural or manmade factors affecting its continued existence*—Contaminants, particularly a large oil spill, could affect the remaining population.

The status of sea otters was evaluated by the IUCN Otter Specialist Group in 2000, and the species was listed by the IUCN as endangered based on criteria A1a, A1c, and A1e (IUCN 1996). Neither the northern subspecies nor the southwest Alaska population was evaluated as a separate taxon. Threats identified at the time were oil pollution, killer whale predation, poaching, and fishery interactions.

In 2001 FWS was petitioned by the Center for Biological Diversity to list the Alaska stock of sea otters as depleted under the MMPA (66 Fed. Reg. 46651), but the petition was denied. The agency found that "the petition does not present substantial information that the petitioned action is warranted. FWS has determined that the statewide population of sea otters in Alaska is larger than presented in the petition. Furthermore, the best available scientific information indicates that multiple stocks of sea otters exist in Alaska" (66 Fed. Reg. 55693). However, with listing of the southwest Alaska population as threatened under the ESA, the taxon qualified as depleted under the MMPA.

Available data

Almost no information is available documenting the recovery of southwest Alaska sea otters prior to the 1950s. From the late 1950s though the 1970s, however, some aerial survey counts were made in various parts of their range. In the 1980s the frequency of surveys increased significantly, including a few range-wide surveys completed during the past 20 years. Direct information on many population parameters (e.g., reproductive rates, mortality, survival rates, and age/sex) is very limited.

No models designed specifically for population viability analysis have been developed for southwest Alaska sea otters.

Current biological status

When sea otters became protected from commercial harvests in 1911, only 13 small remnant populations were known to exist, 6 of them within the bounds of the current southwest Alaska population (Kenyon 1969). With protection, southwest Alaska sea otters increased in abundance and may have been near carrying capacity in the 1980s when numbers were estimated at 55,100 to 73,700 in the Aleutian Islands alone. Surveys in 1992 indicated declines of more than 50 percent at some locations in the Aleutian Islands, and counts made in 2000 showed a further 70 percent decline during that eight-year interval. Additional surveys in 2000 and 2001 in Bristol Bay and along the Alaska Peninsula also showed major declines (Burn and Doroff 2005).

FWS published the most recent SAR for southwest Alaska sea otters in 2002 (see http://www.nmfs .noaa.gov/pr/sars/species.htm). The SAR estimates the size of the population in 2002 as 41,474 and calculates a PBR of 830 animals. It states that the stock is considered strategic because it was a candidate species for ESA listing in 2002. The final rule on ESA listing gives a total population estimate of 41,865 for 2004, which compares to estimates of 94,050 to 128,650 in 1976 (70 Fed. Reg. 46366).

The cause or causes of the decline are not well understood. In good conditions, sea otter populations are capable of increasing at 17 to 20 percent per year (Estes 1990). For the southwest Alaska population there is no evidence for decreased reproduction or limitations due to food availability, which suggests that the current decline is caused by excessive mortality. Relatively small numbers of animals are killed in fishing gear and by Alaska Native subsistence hunters. One hypothesis suggests that increased predation by transient killer whales is the primary cause for the decline (Estes et al. 1998).

Caribbean monk seal (*Monachus tropicalis*) (ESA – endangered; IUCN – extinct; MMPA – depleted)

<u>Distribution and conservation units</u>

The Caribbean monk seal is known only from the Caribbean Sea, Gulf of Mexico, the subtropical coast of Florida, and adjacent subtropical areas, and is geographically isolated from other seals. It is now believed to be extinct (LeBoeuf et al. 1986).

<u>History of evaluation and listing</u>

The Caribbean monk seal is under the jurisdiction of NMFS. Milestones relative to the species' listing include the following:

- Species listed as endangered under the ESPA in 1967.
- Endangered status carried forward under the ESCA in 1970.
- Endangered status carried forward under the ESA in 1973.
- Qualified as depleted under the MMPA in 1973 by virtue of its listing under the ESA.
- Listed as extinct by the IUCN in 1996.

No detailed explanation was given when the Caribbean monk seal was listed as endangered under the ESPA in 1967 (32 Fed. Reg. 4001). Because the species was already listed when the ESA was passed in 1973, a formal analysis of threats and ESA listing factors was not done at that time.

The status of the Caribbean monk seal was most recently evaluated by the IUCN Seal Specialist Group in 1993, which noted that the species was believed to be extinct (Reijnders et al. 1993). In 1996 the IUCN listed the species as extinct (IUCN 1996).

Caribbean monk seals are considered as depleted under the MMPA because of their ESA listing. Their status relative to OSP has not been evaluated.

<u>Available data</u>

Prior to listing under the ESPA in 1967, Caribbean monk seals were very poorly known. No directed studies have been undertaken since 1967. In the 1980s the Marine Mammal Commission supported a survey of fishermen in remote coastal villages on the Island of Hispaniola to determine if there had been any recent sightings, but no sighting reports were obtained (Woods 1987).

<u>Current biological status</u>

Caribbean monk seals were extensively hunted after the arrival of Europeans. The last confirmed sighting of this species in the United States was made in 1922, and the last sighting made anywhere was in 1952 at a remote bank off Honduras (Rice 1973). Although many (e.g., LeBoeuf et al. 1986 and IUCN 1996) consider the species to be extinct, Woods (1987) and Boyd and Standford (1998) present circumstantial evidence that a few individuals may still exist.

Hawaiian monk seal (*Monachus schauinslandi*) (ESA – endangered; IUCN – endangered; MMPA – depleted)

Distribution and conservation units

The Hawaiian monk seal is geographically isolated from other seals and is considered a distinct species with no recognized subspecies (Rice 1998). The species exists as a metapopulation with six primary semi-isolated breeding colonies at Kure Atoll, Midway Atoll, Pearl and Hermes Reef, Lisianski Island, Laysan Island, and French Frigate Shoals. Although these colonies show considerable demographic independence (Ragen and Lavigne 1999) and are considered subpopulations, studies to date have found little genetic difference between them (Kretzmann et al. 1997, 2001). The Hawaiian monk seal occurs only in the Hawaiian archipelago with the majority of the population in the Northwestern Hawaiian Islands (Nihoa Island to Kure Atoll) and a relatively few animals in the main Hawaiian Islands (Hawaii Island to Niihau Island; Ragen and Lavigne 1999).

History of evaluation and listing

The Hawaiian monk seal is under the jurisdiction of NMFS. Milestones relative to the species' listing include the following:

- Species designated as depleted under the MMPA in 1976.
- Species listed as endangered under the ESA in 1976.
- Recovery plan adopted in 1983.
- Listed as endangered by the IUCN in 1996.
- Recovery plan revision currently underway.

The 1976 ESA listing notice (41 Fed. Reg. 33923) included an analysis of the five listing factors that concluded as follows:

   A. *The present or threatened destruction, modification, or curtailment of its habitat or range*—Human activity on beaches formerly used by monk seals has curtailed habitat use, displaced seals, and reduced recruitment. This was identified as the major factor threatening the species.
   B. *Overutilization for commercial, recreational, scientific, or educational purposes*—This factor was not considered applicable.
   C. *Disease or predation*—Shark predation, particularly on weaned pups, was identified as a problem for the reduced population. Disease was not known to be a factor.
   D. *The inadequacy of existing regulatory mechanisms*—Although monk seals were afforded some protection by the Hawaiian Islands National Wildlife Refuge and the MMPA, additional protection, including protection for habitat, could be gained by ESA listing.

E. *Other natural or manmade factors affecting its continued existence*—Vessel traffic and recreational activities in waters where the species occurs may have deleterious effects.

The 1983 recovery plan (Gilmartin 1983) has not been updated although a new plan is currently being developed. The 1983 plan did not identify quantitative criteria for determining when the population had recovered but did describe the following four intermediate goals: (1) stopping the downward trend in numbers in the central and western portions of the species' range; (2) taking action to develop positive growth rates at most or all islands; (3) identifying and preventing human activities that could result in the degradation or destruction of habitats critical to the survival and recovery of the species; and (4) determining the population size that will result in maximum net productivity (Gilmartin 1983). The plan identified important threats as human disturbance (primarily from U.S. Coast Guard and Navy facilities), shark predation, mobbing by adult males, biotoxins (ciguatera), and entanglement in debris. A revision of the recovery plan is currently underway (NMFS in prep.[a]).

The status of the Hawaiian monk seal was most recently evaluated by the IUCN Seal Specialist Group in 1993 (Reijnders et al. 1993). Potential threats to its existence identified at the time were sensitivity to disturbance, male mobbing of adult females, and fishery interactions. In 1996 the IUCN listed the species as endangered based on criterion C2a (IUCN 1996).

NMFS published a proposed rule to designate the Hawaiian monk seal as a depleted species under the MMPA in 1976 (41 Fed. Reg. 24393) prior to its being proposed for ESA listing. The rationale given for a depleted listing was as follows: "Current population estimates indicate that the numbers of monk seals have been decreasing in recent years." No evaluation was done of the population's size relative to OSP. The species was subsequently designated as depleted (41 Fed. Reg. 30120).

Available data

Prior to listing under the ESA in 1976, information on Hawaiian monk seals was very limited. There are a few historical accounts, including some records of seal harvests from the 1800s, and a series of beach counts at various atolls in the Northwestern Hawaiian Islands beginning in 1956. Since 1976 an extensive monitoring program, funded and largely carried out by NMFS, has made Hawaiian monk seals one of the world's best-studied pinnipeds. Major components of the monk seal research program include (1) replicate beach counts at major pupping beaches conducted annually at most colonies since the early 1990s and periodically at many colonies since the 1970s; (2) life history records of a large proportion of individuals flipper-tagged at each major monk seal colony since the early 1980s (including information on age, sex, survivorship, and pupping intervals); (3) satellite tracking studies of seals at different colonies; (4) studies of prey preferences and foraging behavior; and (5) assessments of the health and condition of individuals.

Counts and life history data have been integrated into a population model that gives separate consideration to each major monk seal colony (Harting 2002). The model is suitable for PVA analysis but has not yet been used for that purpose.

Current biological status

The abundance of Hawaiian monk seals before the arrival of Polynesians is not known, but it is likely that the arrival of humans displaced seals from inhabited islands. The first comprehensive counts were made in 1958, and the population declined about 60 percent between then and 2001. Since regular counts began, the subpopulations have shown different dynamics. Counts at most locations declined after 1958, with the exception of French Frigate Shoals. That subpopulation grew rapidly from the early 1960s to the late 1980s, then declined by 70 percent during 1989–2001. Subpopulations at Laysan and Lisianski Islands have been relatively stable since 1990. In contrast, the subpopulation at Kure Atoll grew at an average rate of 5 percent per year after 1983, and the subpopulation at Pearl and Hermes Reef increased at approximately 7 percent per year during 1983–1999. Midway Islands was formerly largely unavailable to monk seals due to military presence, but its subpopulation began to increase after 1990. However, since 2000 all three of the western subpopulations have shown indications of decline. Based on increasing reports of pups being born in the main Hawaiian Islands, it appears that the number of monk seals has been increasing in that area since the 1990s (NMFS in prep.[a]).

NMFS published the most recent SAR for Hawaiian monk seals in 2005 (see http://www.nmfs .noaa.gov/pr/sars/species.htm). The SAR estimates the population size in 2003 as 1,252, and states that since 1993 the population has been declining at a rate of 1.9 percent per year. The SAR states that PBR is undetermined because recovery to MNPL would be unlikely in the foreseeable future if the calculated PBR level of takes was to occur. The Hawaiian monk seal is considered a strategic stock because it is listed as endangered under the ESA.

The declines in Northwestern Hawaiian Islands subpopulations have been attributed to low survival of juvenile seals, but it is not clear why survival has declined. Possible factors include shark predation, entanglement in marine debris, injuries and deaths caused by aggressive male seals, biotoxins, and/or nutritional limitations possibly related to climate cycles and/or commercial lobster fishing. Also, growth and reproductive rates vary among subpopulations, which suggests that some factor such as food availability is limiting reproductive output in some areas (NMFS in prep.[a]).

Guadalupe fur seal (*Arctocephalus townsendi*) (ESA – threatened; IUCN – vulnerable; MMPA – depleted)

Distribution and conservation units

The Guadalupe fur seal is considered to be a distinct species with a single breeding colony at Isla Guadalupe, Mexico (Reijnders et al. 1993, Rice 1998). Currently, a few animals occur in Southern California. Archeological remains indicate the species was taken prehistorically in California by Native Americans, but it is unclear whether breeding colonies ever occurred in California or if the species was ever abundant there (Hanni et al. 1997).

History of evaluation and listing

The Guadalupe fur seal is under the jurisdiction of NMFS. Milestones relative to the species' listing include the following:

- Species listed as endangered under the ESPA in 1967.
- Species listed as threatened under the ESA in 1985.
- Qualified as depleted under the MMPA in 1985 by virtue of listing under the ESA.
- Listed as vulnerable by the IUCN in 1996.

No detailed explanation was given when the Guadalupe fur seal was listed as endangered under the ESPA in 1967 (32 Fed. Reg. 4001). The species was not included on the 1970 list of species considered endangered under the ESCA (35 Fed. Reg. 18319), and there was no explanation given for its omission. This omission was carried forward when the ESA was passed in 1973, and the species therefore remained off the list until it was listed as threatened in 1985 (50 Fed. Reg. 51252). The listing notice included an analysis of the five ESA listing factors that concluded as follows:

A. *The present or threatened destruction, modification, or curtailment of its habitat or range*—Habitat loss has not been the primary factor causing the reduced abundance of the species. Some human activities have the potential to affect their habitat, including offshore oil and gas development, high-intensity sonic booms from the U.S. Air Force's Space Shuttle Program, and disturbance by tourists and fishing vessels.

B. *Overutilization for commercial, recreational, scientific, or educational purposes*—Prior commercial hunting was responsible for significantly reducing population size and range.

C. *Disease or predation*—There was no information available concerning disease or predation.

D. *The inadequacy of existing regulatory mechanisms*—Existing regulations were judged to be providing adequate protection within areas subject to Mexican and U.S. jurisdiction.

E. *Other natural or manmade factors affecting its continued existence*—The potential expansion of several fisheries into waters adjacent to Guadalupe Island could result in fur seal entanglement.

The ESA listing notice also provided the following criteria for determining when the species could be delisted: (1) the population has increased to 30,000 animals; (2) one or more additional rookeries have been established within the historic range; or (3) the population has reached the MNPL. If one or more criteria were met, NMFS would conduct a status review prior to proposing delisting. The status of the Guadalupe fur seal was most recently evaluated by the IUCN Seal Specialist Group in 1993 (Reijnders et al. 1993). The only threat to its existence identified at the time was a possible lack of genetic diversity. In its 1996 Red Book, the IUCN listed the species as vulnerable based on criterion D2 (IUCN 1996).

Guadalupe fur seals are considered as depleted under the MMPA because of their ESA listing. Their status relative to OSP has not been evaluated.

Available data

No breeding colonies of Guadalupe fur seals currently exist in U.S. waters, and a dedicated research program has not been established for this species in the United States. Following their near-extinction in the 1800s, almost no information was collected on the species until the 1950s. Since 1954 sporadic counts have been made at various times of the year at the rookery on Guadalupe Island. Reproduction, mortality, survival rates, and other population parameters are poorly known.

No models designed specifically for population viability analysis have been developed for Guadalupe fur seals.

Current biological status

Guadalupe fur seals were hunted nearly to extinction during the 19th century by commercial sealers and began to recover in the mid-20th century. NMFS published the most recent SAR for Guadalupe fur seals in 2000 (see http://www.nmfs.noaa.gov/pr/sars/species.htm). The SAR gives a 1993 population estimate of 7,408, and states that the population had increased by 13.7 percent per year since the mid-1950s. It calculates a PBR of 104 animals and states that the Guadalupe fur seal is considered a strategic stock because it is listed as threatened under the ESA.

Northern fur seal, eastern Pacific (Pribilof Islands) population (*Callorhinus ursinus*) (ESA – not listed; IUCN – vulnerable; MMPA – depleted)

Distribution and conservation units

The northern fur seal is a distinct species with no recognized subspecies (Rice 1998). There are two populations recognized in U.S. waters: one that pups and breeds only at San Miguel Island in Southern California, and another that pups and breeds on rookeries in the Bering Sea (the eastern Pacific population). Fur seals from the eastern Pacific population mostly use several rookeries on St. George and St. Paul Islands in the Pribilof Islands. They also use a rookery on Bogoslof Island that was established naturally in the 1980s and has grown considerably since then. During the non-breeding season, fur seals range widely throughout the Bering Sea and North Pacific Ocean.

History of evaluation and listing

The northern fur seal is under the jurisdiction of NMFS. Milestones relative to the population's listing include the following:

- Population listed as depleted under the MMPA in 1988.
- Conservation plan adopted in 1993.
- Entire species listed as vulnerable by the IUCN in 1996.
- Conservation plan revision currently underway.

The status of the northern fur seal was most recently evaluated by the IUCN Seal Specialist Group in 1993 (Reijnders et al. 1993). Potential threats to its existence identified at the time were fishery interactions, entanglement in marine debris, and oil and gas exploration and development. In its 1996 Red Book, the IUCN listed the species as vulnerable based on criterion A1b (IUCN 1996). The eastern North Pacific population was not evaluated as a separate taxon.

The Pribilof Islands population of northern fur seals was designated as depleted under the MMPA in 1988 (51 Fed. Reg. 47156) because it had declined to a level less than 50 percent of what it was in the 1950s and there was no evidence that carrying capacity for the species had declined during that time. Therefore the population was determined to be below the lower bound of OSP, which was assumed to be 60 percent of K. The cause of the decline from 1956 to 1968 was thought to be commercial harvests of adult females. Declines after 1976 were thought to be a result of increased mortality of juveniles, perhaps due to entanglement in marine debris and/or changes in prey availability (NMFS 1993).

In 1993 NMFS published the Northern Fur Seal Conservation Plan. The goal of the plan is to "promote recovery of the fur seal population on the Pribilof Islands to a level appropriate to justify removal from MMPA listing" (NMFS 1993). It states that reconsideration of the depleted classification should occur when the sustained abundance (estimated population size or pup counts) reaches 60 percent of the peak historical estimate. The plan identified the following as human-related threats of possible importance at that time: incidental take in fisheries, competition for prey with commercial fisheries, entanglement in marine debris, disturbance and coastal development, toxic substances, and oil spills. A revised draft of the conservation plan is currently in agency review.

Available data

At one time Pribilof fur seals were the most intensely monitored pinniped in the world by virtue of their management under the Fur Seal Treaty of 1911. As part of efforts by Treaty parties—Russia, Japan, the United States, and Great Britain (for Canada)—to determine appropriate harvest levels, estimates of the number of pups, the number of breeding males, and the overall size of the Pribilof Islands fur seal herd were made annually throughout most of the 20th century. Until 1984 cooperative research among the Treaty parties also produced extensive data and analyses of other population parameters (e.g., survival rates by age and sex), at-sea distribution and movements, and feeding habits. The Treaty lapsed in 1984 and subsequently research efforts have decreased substantially. Because of funding limitations, research by NMFS has been limited largely to estimating key population parameters (e.g., the number of pups born and the number of breeding males) every other year in cooperation with the Pribilof Islands Aleut community.

A number of population models have been prepared for Pribilof Islands fur seals, but they have not been used for population viability analysis.

Current biological status

The size of the eastern Pacific population of northern fur seals has fluctuated considerably in the last 100 years, with recovery from overexploitation followed by periods of decrease and increase. As recently as the 1950s it was estimated to number about 2 to 2.5 million. NMFS published the most recent SAR for the population in 2005 (see http://www.nmfs.noaa.gov/pr/sars/species.htm). The SAR estimates the population size as 688,028 (based on an extrapolation from pup counts made in 2004) and calculates a PBR of 14,546 animals. It states that the population is considered a strategic stock because it is listed as depleted under the MMPA. Counts of pups on the Pribilof Islands made during 1998–2004 have shown a steady decline (see http://nmml.afsc.noaa.gov/AlaskaEcosystems/nfshome/pribpup.htm). Potential causes for this most recent decline have not been identified. The colony on Bogoslof Island, however, has increased at a rate of about 12 percent per year since 1997 with pup production in 2005 estimated to exceed 12,000 pups.

Steller sea lion, eastern population (*Eumetopias jubatus*) (ESA – threatened; IUCN – endangered; MMPA – depleted)

Distribution and conservation units

Steller sea lions are a distinct species with no recognized subspecies (Rice 1998). However, two discrete populations are recognized, both of which are currently considered distinct population segments under the ESA and listed separately. The two populations are the eastern population, which includes animals from Cape Suckling, Alaska, east and south to California, and the western population, which includes animals from west of Cape Suckling to Russia. Eastern population Steller sea lions pup and breed on rookeries, and occupy haulouts, in southeast Alaska, British Columbia, Washington, Oregon, and California (NMFS 1995).

History of evaluation and listing

Steller sea lions are under the jurisdiction of NMFS. Milestones relative to the population's listing include the following:

- Advance notice of proposed rulemaking published to designate the entire species as depleted under the MMPA in 1988.
- Entire species listed as threatened under the ESA in 1990.
- Qualified as depleted under the MMPA in 1990 by virtue of listing under the ESA.
- Recovery plan adopted in 1992.
- Species listed as endangered by the IUCN in 1996.
- ESA listing revised in 1997; species split into two populations and the eastern population left as threatened.
- Revised recovery plan released for public review in 2006.

The status of Steller sea lions was first reviewed in 1988 (55 Fed. Reg. 16299). The review concluded that the number of adult and juvenile Steller sea lions counted in southwest Alaska had declined by at least 52 percent from 1956–1960 to 1985. Potential causes of the decline being investigated at the time of the review included fishery interactions, environmental changes, diseases, contaminants, predation, and commercial and subsistence harvests.

In 1990 the Steller sea lion was listed as threatened under the ESA throughout its range because NMFS determined that, given is declining trend, it was likely to become an endangered species within the foreseeable future (55 Fed. Reg. 49204). The 1990 listing notice included an analysis of the five ESA listing factors that concluded as follows:

A. *The present or threatened destruction, modification, or curtailment of its habitat or range*—Activities that result in disturbance or changes in prey availability could be affecting suitability of habitat.
B. *Overutilization for commercial, recreational, scientific, or educational purposes*—Commercial harvests of pups prior to the 1970s could explain early parts of the declines in some areas. Subsistence takes by Alaska Natives have been too small to have caused the overall decline.
C. *Disease or predation*—Disease was unlikely to have been a significant factor in the decline. Killer whale predation was probably unimportant when the sea lion population was high but could exacerbate a decline once numbers have been reduced.
D. *The inadequacy of existing regulatory mechanisms*—The MMPA prohibits most taking and has a mechanism to limit incidental take by fisheries. No inadequacies were noted.
E. *Other natural or manmade factors affecting its continued existence*—Incidental take in fisheries and intentional shooting may have had some impact but cannot explain the overall decline.

The 1992 Final Recovery Plan for Steller Sea Lions states its goal as "to promote the recovery of the Steller sea lion population to a level appropriate to justify removal from ESA listings" (NMFS 1992). The plan includes quantitative criteria that the recovery team recommended for reclassification and delisting based on counts and trends in counts of pup and non-pup Steller sea lions in the principal area of decline and elsewhere. However, the approved plan states that NMFS would not implement those recommendations, but instead would develop final criteria after further analyses, including a population viability analysis. Human-related threats identified in the plan were subsistence harvests, fishery-related taking, competition for food with commercial fisheries, toxic substances, entanglement in debris, and disturbance.

NMFS published a second status review of Steller sea lions in 1995. The review concluded that the species should be split into two populations. The eastern population was predicted to persist for the foreseeable future because its population trend was stable or increasing. No evaluation was done of ESA listing factors and no specific threats to the population were identified (NMFS 1995).

In 1997 NMFS revised the ESA listing to reflect new information on the species' population structure and status. It retained the classification of threatened for the eastern population based on the following rationale: "The eastern population segment has exhibited a stable population trend for the last 15 years; however, NMFS believes that the large decline within the overall U.S. population threatens the continued existence of the entire species. This is particularly true, since the underlying causes of the decline remain unknown and thus unpredictable. Therefore, despite the apparent stability of the eastern population segment, NMFS is maintaining a threatened listing for this portion of the geographic range" (62 Fed. Reg. 24345).

The 1997 listing notice included an analysis of the five ESA listing factors for the eastern population that concluded as follows:

A. *The present or threatened destruction, modification, or curtailment of its habitat or range*—Human disturbance may have had an effect at certain rookeries in Oregon and California, and changes may have occurred in prey resources in California due to natural cycles, fisheries, and toxic substances.
B. *Overutilization for commercial, recreational, scientific, or educational purposes*—Commercial harvest and illegal shooting may have been significant factors in the past but are not considered major factors at this time. Utilization for scientific or educational purposes has not been a significant factor.
C. *Disease or predation*—Neither disease nor predation is considered a significant factor currently affecting the population.
D. *The inadequacy of existing regulatory mechanisms*—The listing states, "A final determination with respect to whether existing regulatory mechanisms are adequate is difficult to make, given the lack of a clear cause of the decline."
E. *Other natural or manmade factors affecting its continued existence*—Removals from the eastern population due to incidental takes in fisheries and Alaska Native subsistence hunting are low. Concern has been expressed about the possible adverse effects of anthropogenic contaminants on the health and productivity of animals in California.

In May 2006 NMFS released a revised draft Steller Sea Lion Recovery Plan for public review (71 Fed. Reg. 29919).

The status of the Steller sea lion was most recently evaluated by the IUCN Seal Specialist Group in 1993 (Reijnders et al. 1993). Potential threats to its existence identified at the time were deliberate killing by fishermen, incidental take by fisheries, reduced food supply, and disease. In its 1996 Red Book, the IUCN listed the entire species as endangered based on criterion A1b (IUCN 1996). The status of the eastern population was not evaluated separately.

In 1988 NMFS published an advance notice of proposed rulemaking to list Steller sea lions as depleted under the MMPA, citing results of its status review and stating that "the current population may be below 50 percent of historic carrying capacity and below the lower bound of OSP for this population" (55 Fed. Reg. 16299). NMFS did not follow through on the depletion designation but instead proceeded to list Steller sea lions under the ESA. Therefore, the eastern population of Steller sea lions is considered as depleted under the MMPA because it is listed under the ESA. Its status relative to OSP has not been evaluated.

Available data

The basic population data available for Steller sea lions are counts of animals (usually both pups and non-pups) on rookeries during the pupping and breeding season. For California and British Columbia, some counts are available starting in the early 1900s. For Oregon and southeast Alaska, systematic counts began in the mid to late 1970s. Since sea lions were listed under the ESA in 1990, all major rookeries have been counted at regular intervals, usually every other year.

Prior to ESA listing, Steller sea lion research was funded and conducted primarily by NMFS and State agencies, especially the Alaska Department of Fish and Game (ADFG). After listing, Congress began to annually appropriate additional funds to investigate causes of the population's decline. Initially funding was earmarked primarily to support work by NMFS and ADFG, but later it was expanded to include a number of universities and other research and management agencies. Data have been gathered on a variety of subjects including distribution, abundance, movements, stock structure, vital parameters, life history, foraging ecology, behavior, physiology, contaminants, predation, and disease. The majority of effort has gone to studies of the western population, but significant data have been gathered also for the eastern population.

A model that can be used for population viability analysis has recently been developed for Steller sea lions (NMFS in prep.[b]).

Current biological status

NMFS published the most recent SAR for the eastern population of Steller sea lions in 2005 (see http://www.nmfs.noaa.gov/pr/sars/species.htm) . The SAR estimates total abundance as 44,996 (based on pup counts made in 2002) and calculates a PBR of 1,967 animals. It states that the eastern population of Steller sea lions is considered a strategic stock because it is listed as threatened under the ESA. Based on pup counts, Pitcher et al. (2007) estimate that the eastern population's abundance increased at a rate of 3.1 percent per year from the 1970s to 2005.

Steller sea lion, western population (*Eumetopias jubatus*) (ESA – endangered; IUCN – endangered; MMPA – depleted)

Distribution and conservation units

Steller sea lions are a distinct species with no recognized subspecies (Rice 1998). However, two discrete populations are recognized, both of which are currently considered distinct population segments under the ESA and listed separately. The two populations are the eastern population, which includes animals from Cape Suckling, Alaska, east and south to California, and the western population, which includes animals from west of Cape Suckling to Russia. Steller sea lions range around the rim of the North Pacific Ocean from California through Alaska and to Russia and Japan

(NMFS 1992). Western sea lions pup and breed on rookeries, and occupy haulouts, in central and western Alaska, eastern Russia, and northern Japan (NMFS 1995).

History of evaluation and listing

Steller sea lions are under the jurisdiction of NMFS. Milestones relative to the population's listing include the following:

- Advance notice of proposed rulemaking published to designate the entire species as depleted under the MMPA in 1988.
- Entire species listed as threatened under the ESA in 1990.
- Qualified as depleted under the MMPA in 1990 by virtue of listing under the ESA.
- Recovery plan adopted in 1992.
- Species listed as endangered by the IUCN in 1996.
- ESA listing revised in 1997; species split into two populations and the western population reclassified as endangered.
- Revised recovery plan released for public review in 2006.

The status of Steller sea lions was first reviewed in 1988 (55 Fed. Reg. 16299). The review concluded that the number of adult and juvenile Steller sea lions counted in southwest Alaska had declined by at least 52 percent from 1956–1960 to 1985. Potential causes of the decline being investigated at the time of the review included fishery interactions, environmental changes, diseases, contaminants, predation, and commercial and subsistence harvests.

In 1990 the Steller sea lion was listed as threatened under the ESA because NMFS determined that it was likely to become an endangered species within the foreseeable future, given its ongoing decline (55 Fed. Reg. 49204). The 1990 listing notice included an analysis of the five ESA listing factors that concluded as follows:

- A. *The present or threatened destruction, modification, or curtailment of its habitat or range*—Activities that result in disturbance or changes in prey availability could be affecting suitability of habitat.
- B. *Overutilization for commercial, recreational, scientific, or educational purposes*—Prior commercial harvests of pups could explain early parts of the declines in some areas. Alaska Native subsistence takes have been too small to have caused the overall decline.
- C. *Disease or predation*—Disease was unlikely to have been a significant factor in the decline. Killer whale predation was probably unimportant when the sea lion population was high but could exacerbate a decline once numbers have been reduced.
- D. *The inadequacy of existing regulatory mechanisms*—The MMPA prohibits most taking and has a mechanism to limit incidental take by fisheries. No inadequacies were noted.
- E. *Other natural or manmade factors affecting its continued existence*—Incidental take in fisheries and intentional shooting may have had some impact but cannot explain the overall decline.

The 1992 Final Recovery Plan for Steller Sea Lions states its goal as "to promote the recovery of the Steller sea lion population to a level appropriate to justify removal from ESA listings" (NMFS 1992). The plan includes quantitative criteria that the recovery team recommended for reclassification and delisting based on counts and trends in counts of pup and non-pup Steller sea lions in the principal area of decline and elsewhere. However, the approved plan states that NMFS would not implement those recommendations but instead would develop final criteria after further analyses, including a population viability analysis. Human-related threats identified in the plan were subsistence harvests, fishery-related taking, competition for food with commercial fisheries, toxic substances, entanglement in debris, and disturbance.

NMFS published a second status review of Steller sea lions in 1995. The review concluded that the species should be split into two populations. Models using historical trends predicted that the western population could be reduced to very low levels within 100 years. The review concluded that the proximate cause of the population decline was primarily a reduction in juvenile survival, and that disease and changes in prey abundance were the most likely causes of that change. No evaluation was done of ESA listing factors (NMFS 1995).

In 1997 NMFS revised the ESA listing to reflect new information on the species' population structure and status. It changed the classification of the western population to endangered based on the following rationale: "Available data on population trends indicate that the western population segment of Steller sea lions is in danger of extinction throughout all or a significant part of its range. This population had exhibited a precipitous, large population decline at the time that the Steller sea lion was listed as a threatened species in 1990 and has continued to decline since the listing. Therefore, the western population segment of Steller sea lions is reclassified as an endangered species under the ESA" (62 Fed. Reg. 24345).

The 1997 listing notice included an analysis of the five ESA listing factors for the western population that concluded as follows:

A. *The present or threatened destruction, modification, or curtailment of its habitat or range*—There is no evidence that habitat factors are significant issues.
B. *Overutilization for commercial, recreational, scientific, or educational purposes*—Commercial harvest and illegal shooting may have been significant factors in past declines but are not a major cause of recent population changes. Utilization for scientific or educational purposes has not been a significant factor.
C. *Disease or predation*—Disease and predation are not considered significant factors currently affecting the population.
D. *The inadequacy of existing regulatory mechanisms*—The listing states, "A final determination with respect to whether existing regulatory mechanisms are adequate is difficult to make, given the lack of a clear cause of the decline."
E. *Other natural or manmade factors affecting its continued existence*—Incidental catch in fisheries may have been a contributing factor to declines in some areas during certain periods. Alaska Native subsistence hunting may become significant if the population continues to decline

and harvests continue at current levels. There is evidence that limitations in food availability, due either to commercial fishing or environmental changes, may be a factor in the ongoing decline. Concern has been expressed about possible effects of contaminants, but their possible significance is unknown.

In May 2006 NMFS released a revised draft Steller Sea Lion Recovery Plan for public review (71 Fed. Reg. 29919).

The status of the Steller sea lion was most recently evaluated by the IUCN Seal Specialist Group in 1993 (Reijnders et al. 1993). Potential threats to its existence identified at the time were deliberate killing by fishermen, incidental take by fisheries, reduced food supply, and disease. In its 1996 Red Book, the IUCN listed the entire species as endangered based on criterion A1b (IUCN 1996). The status of the western population was not evaluated separately.

In 1988 NMFS published an advance notice of proposed rulemaking to list Steller sea lions as depleted under the MMPA citing results of its status review and stating that "the current population may be below 50 percent of historic carrying capacity and below the lower bound of OSP for this population" (55 Fed. Reg. 16299). NMFS did not follow through on the depletion designation but instead proceeded with listing Steller sea lions under the ESA. Therefore, the western population of Steller sea lions is considered as depleted under the MMPA because it is listed under the ESA. Its status relative to OSP has not been evaluated.

Available data

The basic population data available for Steller sea lions are counts of animals (usually both pups and non-pups) on rookeries during the pupping and breeding season. The first systematic counts of the western population were made in the Gulf of Alaska and Aleutian Islands in the late 1950s. Subsequent counts were made during 1975–1979, 1984–1985, and 1989–1990. Since sea lions were listed under the ESA in 1990, all major rookeries have been counted at regular intervals, usually every other year.

Prior to ESA listing, research on the western stock of Steller sea lions was funded and conducted primarily by NMFS and ADFG. During 1975–1979 a major research project funded by the Outer Continental Shelf Environmental Assessment Program produced detailed information on the distribution, abundance, and life history of sea lions, principally in the Gulf of Alaska. After ESA listing, Congress began to appropriate additional funds annually to investigate the population's decline. Initially, funding was earmarked primarily to support work by NMFS and ADFG, but later it expanded to include a number of universities and other research and management agencies. Data have been gathered on a variety of subjects including distribution, abundance, movements, stock structure, vital parameters, life history, foraging ecology, behavior, physiology, contaminants, predation, and disease. The majority of effort has gone to studies of the western population, and a huge amount of information has been collected.

A model that can be used for population viability analysis has recently been developed for Steller sea lions (NMFS in prep.[b]).

Current biological status

NMFS published the most recent SAR for the western population of Steller sea lions in 2005 (see http://www.nmfs.noaa.gov/pr/sars/species.htm) . The SAR gives a minimum abundance of 38,513 (based on counts made in 2001–2004) and states that the population declined by 3.1 percent per year from 1991 to 2004. It calculates a PBR of 231 animals and states that the population is considered a strategic stock because it is listed as endangered under the ESA. Trend counts for the western Steller sea lion population declined by 81 percent from 109,880 in the late 1970s to 20,563 in 2004. The most recent count data suggest that the decline may have stopped and that sea lion numbers are increasing slowly in some regions (see http://nmml.afsc.noaa.gov/AlaskaEcosystems/sslhome/decline.htm).

Although reproductive and mortality rates are poorly known, the proximate cause of the decline is likely to be poor survival, especially of juveniles (NRC 2003). One theory has proposed that much of the mortality may be due to killer whale predation (Springer et al. 2003). The SAR notes that another possibility is that prey availability in sea lion foraging area has been reduced by commercial fishing and/or climate changes.

Blue whale (*Balaenoptera musculus*) (ESA – endangered; IUCN – endangered; MMPA – depleted)

Distribution and conservation units

The blue whale is a cosmopolitan species with four recognized subspecies, one of which occurs in the Northern Hemisphere (Rice 1998). Current information suggests that multiple populations occur within different ocean basins. The Recovery Plan for the Blue Whale discusses North Atlantic and North Pacific populations separately (NMFS 1998a). For purposes of SARs required by the MMPA, NMFS has identified three stocks—western North Atlantic, eastern North Pacific (formerly called California/Mexico), and western North Pacific (formerly called Hawaii). Blue whales range widely in the North Atlantic and North Pacific from the subtropics to the subarctic, and are most common in offshore waters (Perry et al. 1999).

History of evaluation and listing

The blue whale is under the jurisdiction of NMFS. Milestones relative to the species' listing include the following:

- Species listed as endangered under the ESCA in 1970.
- Endangered status carried forward under the ESA in 1973.

- Qualified as depleted under the MMPA in 1973 by virtue of its listing under the ESA.
- North Pacific population listed as lower risk and North Atlantic population as vulnerable by the IUCN in 1996.
- Recovery plan adopted in 1998.

No detailed explanation was given when the blue whale was listed as endangered under the ESCA in 1970 (35 Fed. Reg. 18319). Because the species was already listed when the ESA was passed in 1973, a formal analysis of threats and ESA listing factors was not done at that time.

The Recovery Plan for the Blue Whale states its goal as "to promote the recovery of blue whale populations so that it becomes appropriate to remove them from the list of Endangered and Threatened Wildlife under the Endangered Species Act" (NMFS 1998a). Threats identified in the plan were collisions with vessels, entanglement in fishing gear, reduced food availability due to habitat degradation, and disturbance from low-frequency noise.

The most recent review of the status of blue whales under the ESA was published in 1999 (Perry et al. 1999). The review states, "Any reevaluation of blue whale status awaits the collection of more reliable information on stock structure, distribution and migration patterns, trends in abundance, causes of mortality, and factors affecting the recovery of blue whale stocks, as well as the development of objective delisting criteria." It recommends that the classification status of all blue whale stocks should remain as endangered. ESA listing factors identified in the status review as possibly influencing recovery were destruction or modification of habitat (offshore oil and gas development and noise from vessel traffic); overutilization (whale-watching, scientific research, photography, and associated vessel traffic); and other factors (vessel collisions and entanglement in fishing gear).

In 1996 the IUCN listed the blue whale species as endangered based on criteria A1a, A1b, and A1d (IUCN 1996). The North Atlantic population was listed as vulnerable based on criterion D1, and the North Pacific population was listed as lower-risk, conservation-dependent.[3] The status of blue whales was most recently evaluated by the IUCN Cetacean Specialist Group in 2003 (Reeves et al. 2003). The report states that at the time there were no well-identified threats from human activities but notes that blue whales could be susceptible to changes in ocean productivity such as might result from climate change.

Blue whales are considered as depleted under the MMPA because of their ESA listing. Their status relative to OSP has not been evaluated.

---

[3] The category of "lower-risk, conservation-dependent" is no longer in use, but the categorization for this taxon has not been changed because a formal reassessment of status has not been done.

<u>Available data</u>

Prior to listing under the ESCA in 1970, information on blue whales in U.S. waters was limited almost exclusively to historical whaling records and reports of scattered opportunistic sightings. Since then, there had been almost no directed studies to assess the status of blue whales in U.S. waters until the past few years. Recent studies include seasonal surveys to (1) count and photo-identify blue whales on feeding grounds in the eastern North Pacific (i.e., off the coast of California, Oregon, and Washington); (2) track the movements of whales using satellite tags after they leave waters off California; and (3) assess blue whale distribution and stock structure in the North Pacific and North Atlantic Oceans using acoustic recordings of their calls. Information on blue whales in U.S. waters, particularly in the North Atlantic Ocean, is generally very poor.

No models designed specifically for population viability analysis have been developed for blue whale populations in U.S. waters.

<u>Current biological status</u>

Blue whale populations in both the North Atlantic and North Pacific were greatly reduced by commercial whaling during the early and mid-1900s (NMFS 1998a). Gambell (1976) gives pre-exploitation population estimates of 4,900 blue whales for the entire North Pacific and 1,100 to 1,500 for the entire North Atlantic, but those estimates are considered speculative and statistically unreliable (Perry et al. 1999). NMFS published the most recent SARs for the western North Atlantic stock of blue whales in 2002 and the eastern and western North Pacific stocks in 2005 (see http://www.nmfs.noaa.gov/pr/sars/species.htm) . Stock status parameters given in the SARs are shown here.

Stock name	Abundance	PBR	Trend	Classification
Western North Atlantic	No reliable estimate	Unknown	Insufficient data	Strategic
Eastern North Pacific	1,744[*]	1.4	Possibly increasing	Strategic
Western North Pacific	No reliable estimate	Unknown	Insufficient data	Strategic

[*]A more recent analysis of ship survey data gave an estimate of 2,994 blue whales off Baja California, California, Oregon, and Washington during 1991–1996 (Calambokidis and Barlow 2004).

Bowhead whale, western Arctic population (*Balaena mysticetus*) (ESA – endangered; IUCN – lower risk; MMPA – depleted)

<u>Distribution and conservation units</u>

Bowhead whales are currently considered a single species with no identified subspecies (Rice 1998). Five populations are recognized for management purposes, only one of which, the western Arctic (also called Bering Sea or Bering–Chukchi–Beaufort Seas) population, occurs in U.S. waters (Shelden and Rugh 1995). Western Arctic bowhead whales range seasonally throughout the northern Bering, Chukchi, and Beaufort Seas, usually in association with sea ice.

History of evaluation and listing

The western Arctic bowhead whale is under the jurisdiction of NMFS. Milestones relative to the species' listing include the following:

- Species listed as endangered under the ESCA in 1970.
- Endangered status carried forward under the ESA in 1973.
- Qualified as depleted under the MMPA in 1973 by virtue of its listing under the ESA.
- Listed as lower-risk, conservation-dependent by the IUCN in 1996.

No detailed explanation was given when the bowhead whale was listed as endangered under the ESCA in 1970 (35 Fed. Reg. 18319). Because the species was already listed when the ESA was passed in 1973, a formal analysis of threats and ESA listing factors was not done at that time. A recovery plan has not been prepared for bowhead whales.

A review of the status of bowhead whales under the ESA was conducted in 1995. It concluded that the western Arctic stock was relatively large and had been increasing (Shelden and Rugh 1995). Although bowhead whales are killed by subsistence hunters, attacked by killer whales, and may die as a result of entanglement in fishing gear, the principal threat to the population identified in the review was impacts associated with offshore oil and gas development. No analysis was done of ESA listing factors, and the review made no recommendations on the population's status under ESA because objective criteria for downlisting or delisting had not been developed.

Shelden et al. (2001) proposed methods for developing objective criteria to classify species under the ESA, using bowhead whales as a case study. They reviewed the five ESA listing factors and concluded that they do not provide compelling reasons for listing western Arctic bowhead whales. They then applied a modeling approach developed by Gerber and DeMaster (1999) and concluded that, based on those results, the western Arctic population should be delisted under the ESA.

In 1996 the IUCN listed the western Arctic bowhead whale population as lower-risk, conservation-dependent[4] (IUCN 1996). The status of bowhead whales was most recently evaluated by the IUCN Cetacean Specialist Group in 2003 (Reeves et al. 2003). Its report notes that the western Arctic population has been growing for the past 20 years despite subsistence hunting. No potential threats to its existence were identified at the time.

The western Arctic bowhead whale population is designated as depleted under the MMPA because of its ESA listing. The population's status relative to OSP has not been evaluated. Shelden and Rugh

---

[4] See note 3 above.

(1995) provided an estimate of the lower end of the OSP range as 6,500 to 10,500, based on an estimated initial stock size of 10,945 to 17,431 (IWC 1995) and an assumption that the MNPL is 60 percent of K.

Available data

Prior to listing under the ESCA in 1970, information on bowhead whales in U.S. waters was limited almost exclusively to historical whaling records and reports of scattered opportunistic sightings. Since 1978 directed studies of western Arctic bowhead whales have been funded and conducted by NMFS, Minerals Management Service, Alaska Eskimo Whaling Commission, and North Slope Borough. The western Arctic bowhead whale population is now one of the best-studied large whale populations in the world. Principal research efforts have included periodic counts of migrating whales as they pass along the ice edge near Point Barrow to estimate the size of the population. Counts have been supplemented by acoustic surveys to account for whales passing by the counting stations beyond visual range. Population size also was estimated from aerial surveys in 1985 and 1986 using aerial photographs of whales and capture-recapture methods. The results have provided a good estimate of population size and trends over the past two decades. More recent studies include satellite-tracking work, genetic analyses to assess stock structure, and additional aerial photogrammetry studies to estimate stock size using mark-recapture methods. A number of studies have been done to evaluate the potential impacts of human activities, particularly noise from oil and gas exploration and development, on western Arctic bowhead whales.

A population viability analysis done for bowhead whales concluded that the western Arctic population should be delisted under the ESA (Shelden et al. 2001).

Current biological status

Bowhead whale numbers were severely reduced throughout the Arctic by commercial whaling in the 1800s and early 1900s. The pre-exploitation abundance of the western Arctic population was estimated to be 23,000 by Woodby and Botkin (1993) and 10,945 to 17,431 by the International Whaling Commission (1995). NMFS published the most recent SAR for the western Arctic population of bowhead whales in 2005 (see www.nmfs.noaa.gov/pr/sars/species.htm). The SAR estimates the population size as 10,545 and increasing at 3.4 percent per year. It calculates a PBR of 95 animals and states that western Arctic bowheads are considered a strategic stock because they are listed as endangered under the ESA.

The primary source of human-caused mortality for this population is subsistence hunting by Alaska Natives. Such hunting is closely regulated both by a cooperative agreement between NMFS and the Alaska Eskimo Whaling Commission and by the IWC.

Fin whale (*Balaenoptera physalus*) (ESA – endangered; IUCN – endangered; MMPA – depleted)

<u>Distribution and conservation units</u>

The fin whale is a cosmopolitan species with two recognized subspecies: one in the Northern Hemisphere and the other in the Southern Hemisphere (Rice 1998). Animals in the North Atlantic and North Pacific are likely isolated, and the draft Recovery Plan for the Fin Whale and Sei Whale deals with them as separate populations (NMFS 1998b). For purposes of SARs required by the MMPA, NMFS has identified four stocks—western North Atlantic, California-Oregon-Washington, northeast Pacific, and Hawaii. Fin whales are an oceanic species that seasonally move north or south. In general, wintering areas and migration routes are poorly known (Perry et al. 1999).

<u>History of evaluation and listing</u>

The fin whale is under the jurisdiction of NMFS. Milestones relative to the species' listing include the following:

- Species listed as endangered under the ESCA in 1970.
- Endangered status carried forward under the ESA in 1973.
- Qualified as depleted under the MMPA in 1973 by virtue of its listing under the ESA.
- Listed as endangered by the IUCN in 1996.
- Draft recovery plan prepared in 1998 but not adopted.
- Draft recovery plan released for public review in 2006.

No detailed explanation was given when the fin whale was listed as endangered under the ESCA in 1970 (35 Fed. Reg. 18319). Because the species was already listed when the ESA was passed in 1973, a formal analysis of threats and ESA listing factors was not done at that time.

A draft Recovery Plan for the Fin Whale and Sei Whale was prepared by NMFS in 1998, but no action was taken to adopt it. The draft plan stated that its goal was "to promote recovery of all fin and sei whale populations to levels at which it becomes appropriate to downlist them from endangered to threatened status, and ultimately to remove them from the list of Endangered and Threatened Wildlife and Plants, under the provisions of the ESA" (NMFS 1998b). Threats identified in the plan were vessel interactions (collisions and noise), entanglement in fishing gear, disturbance from low-frequency noise, and hunting. In July 2006 NMFS released a revised draft Recovery Plan for the Fin Whale for public review (71 Fed. Reg. 38385).

The most recent status review of fin whales under the ESA was published in 1999 (Perry et al. 1999). The review states, "Any reevaluation of fin whale status awaits the collection of more reliable information on stock structure, distribution and migration patterns, trends in abundance, causes of mortality, and factors influencing the recovery of fin whale stocks, as well as the development of objective delisting criteria." It makes no specific recommendation for reclassifying or delisting the species under the ESA. The ESA listing factors identified in the status review as possibly influencing recovery were destruction or modification of habitat (offshore oil and gas development); overutilization (whale-watching, scientific research, photography and associated vessel traffic, West Greenland and Icelandic harvests); disease (nematode infestations); and other factors (vessel collisions).

In 1996 the IUCN listed fin whales worldwide as endangered based on criteria A1a, A1b, and A1d (IUCN 1996). Individual populations were not evaluated separately. The status of fin whales was most recently evaluated by the IUCN Cetacean Specialist Group in 2003 (Reeves et al. 2003). Ship strikes were identified as a potential threat in that review.

Fin whales are considered as depleted under the MMPA because of their ESA listing. No formal evaluation has been conducted of their status relative to OSP.

Available data

Prior to listing under the ESCA in 1970, information on fin whales in U.S. waters was limited almost exclusively to data associated with efforts to manage commercial whaling (e.g., catch and sighting records and tag recovery). Since 1970 there have been very few studies directed specifically at fin whales in U.S. waters. Available information is limited largely to sighting data collected during aerial and shipboard surveys for marine mammals, stranding records, and a few photo-identification studies in localized areas. Recordings of fin whale calls have been analyzed to assess their distribution in the North Pacific, and fin whale sightings along the eastern United States were analyzed as part of a series of marine mammal and turtle surveys supported by the Bureau of Land Management between 1979 and 1981. For populations in U.S. waters, information on abundance, population dynamics, and trends is very limited.

No models designed specifically for population viability analysis have been developed for fin whale populations in U.S. waters.

Current biological status

Populations of fin whales in both the North Atlantic and North Pacific were greatly reduced by commercial whaling during the early and mid-1900s (NMFS 1998b). Pre-exploitation population estimates for fin whales are 42,000 to 45,000 for the entire North Pacific and 30,000 to 50,000 for the entire North Atlantic (Perry et al. 1999). NMFS published the most recent SARs for the California-Oregon-Washington stock of fin whales in 2003 and for the western North Atlantic, the northeastern Pacific, and the Hawaii stocks in 2005 (see http://www.nmfs.noaa.gov/pr/sars/species.htm). Stock status parameters given in the SARs are shown on the opposite page.

Stock name	Abundance	PBR	Trend	Classification
Western North Atlantic	2,814	4.7	Insufficient data	Strategic
California-Oregon-Washington	3,279	15.0	Possibly increasing	Strategic
Northeastern Pacific	5,703	11.4	Insufficient data	Strategic
Hawaii	174	0.2	Insufficient data	Strategic

Humpback whale (*Megaptera novaeangliae*) (ESA – endangered; IUCN – vulnerable; MMPA – depleted)

Distribution and conservation units

Humpback whales occur in all the world's oceans except the Arctic Ocean and are currently considered a single species with no recognized subspecies (Rice 1998). They typically feed in summer at higher latitudes and winter at lower latitudes where they calve and breed. Based on whaling records, photographic resightings, and genetics data, about a dozen populations have been identified worldwide, with geographically distinct calving and breeding areas (Perry et al. 1999). The Recovery Plan for the Humpback Whale considers three populations in U.S. waters: one in the western North Atlantic, another in the central North Pacific, and a third in the eastern North Pacific (NMFS 1991a). In at least some instances, humpback whales show fidelity to specific summer feeding areas (Perry et al. 1999), and those feeding aggregations also may comprise important conservation units. For purposes of preparing SARs required by the MMPA, NMFS has identified four stocks—Gulf of Maine (formerly called the western North Atlantic stock), eastern North Pacific (formerly called the California-Oregon-Washington-Mexico stock), central North Pacific, and western North Pacific.

History of evaluation and listing

The humpback whale is under the jurisdiction of NMFS. Milestones relative to the species' listing include the following:

- Species listed as endangered under the ESCA in 1970.
- Endangered status carried forward under the ESA in 1973.
- Qualified as depleted under the MMPA in 1973 by virtue of its listing under the ESA.
- Recovery plan adopted in 1991.
- Listed as vulnerable by the IUCN in 1996.

No detailed explanation was given when the humpback whale was listed as endangered under the ESCA in 1970 (35 Fed. Reg. 18319). Because the species was already listed when the ESA was passed in 1973, a formal analysis of threats and ESA listing factors was not done at that time.

The Final Recovery Plan for the Humpback Whale states its long-term goal as "to increase humpback whale populations to at least 60 percent of the number existing before commercial exploitation or of current environmental carrying capacity" and its interim goal as "a doubling of extant populations within the next 20 years" (NMFS 1991a). Threats identified in the plan were subsistence hunting, entanglement in fishing gear, collisions with vessels, acoustic disturbance, habitat degradation, and competition with humans for food resources.

The most recent review of the status of humpback whales under the ESA was published in 1999 (Perry et al. 1999). It states as follows: "Assuming that abundance levels are accurate and continue to increase, anthropogenic threats are reduced, adequate monitoring plans are developed and implemented, and information on population trends continue to be collected, the western North Atlantic and central North Pacific stocks should be considered for downlisting to threatened status." This recommendation was apparently based in part on an unpublished paper by Gerber and DeMaster (1997) that developed possible classification criteria for humpback whales based on abundance, trends in abundance, changes in distribution, and regulatory status. ESA listing factors identified in the status review as possibly influencing recovery were destruction or modification of habitat (vessel traffic, oil and gas exploration); channel dredging and coastal development (western North Atlantic stock only); overutilization (whale-watching, scientific research, photography, and associated vessel traffic); hunting by whalers near West Greenland and St. Vincent and the Grenadines (western North Atlantic stock only); disease (saxitoxin—western North Atlantic stock only); and other factors (entanglement in fishing gear, vessel collisions, and human depletion of fish stocks—western North Atlantic stock only). Subsequently, Gerber and DeMaster (1999) proposed quantitative criteria for classifying humpback whales under the ESA and concluded as follows: "It was determined that the best estimates of current abundance for the central population of North Pacific humpback whales were larger than the estimated threshold for endangered status but less than the estimated threshold for threatened status. If accepted by the responsible management agency, this analysis would be consistent with a recommendation to downlist the central stock of humpback whales to a status of threatened, whereas the status of eastern and western stocks would remain endangered."

In 1996 the IUCN listed humpback whales worldwide as vulnerable based on criteria A1a and A1d (IUCN 1996). Individual populations were not evaluated separately. The status of humpback whales was most recently evaluated by the IUCN Cetacean Specialist Group in 2003 (Reeves et al. 2003). Potential threats identified in the review include ship collisions, entanglement in fishing gear, and noise disturbance, but the report notes that humpbacks seem able to tolerate living in close proximity to many human activities.

Humpback whales are considered as depleted under the MMPA because of their ESA listing. Their status relative to OSP has not been evaluated.

Available data

Prior to listing under the ESCA in 1970, information on humpback whales in U.S. waters was limited almost exclusively to data associated with efforts to manage commercial whaling (e.g., catch and sighting records and tag recovery). Since then, a considerable amount of information has been gathered on humpback biology, especially in their nearshore calving and feeding areas. Some of this work has been funded and conducted by NMFS, but large contributions have been made by many other organizations and individuals. The development of methods to identify individuals from markings on their flukes has produced data on stock structure, movements, and vital rates. Photo-identification data have also been used to estimate population sizes using mark-recapture methods. Information on mortality has been collected through regional stranding programs. Genetic analyses of biopsy samples have been used to examine population structure. A number of animals have been tagged with satellite-linked transmitters that have produced data on movements and behavior. Additional data on distribution and abundance has been collected during aerial and shipboard surveys for other marine mammals.

During the 1980s and early 1990s a number of researchers studied humpback whales, often independently collecting data in small parts of a population's range. However, in 1992–1993 investigators from several institutions and several countries came together to conduct a cooperative international study called YoNAH (Years of the North Atlantic Humpback), which produced a comprehensive picture of the biology of North Atlantic humpback whales. More recently a similar international program called SPLASH (Structure of Populations, Levels of Abundance, and Status of Humpbacks) has been initiated to assess and sample humpback whales throughout the North Pacific Ocean.

No models designed specifically for population viability analysis have been developed for humpback whale populations in U.S. waters.

Current biological status

All humpback whale populations in the Northern Hemisphere were reduced by commercial whaling between the mid-1800s and mid-1900s (NMFS 1998b). The pre-exploitation abundance of humpback whales for the entire North Pacific Ocean has been estimated as 15,000, but there is no comparable estimate for the North Atlantic (Perry et al. 1999). NMFS published the most recent SARs for humpbacks in the Gulf of Maine, the eastern North Pacific, the central North Pacific, and the western North Pacific in 2005 (see http://www.nmfs.noaa.gov/pr/sars/species.htm). Stock status parameters given in the SARs are shown on the following page.

Stock name	Abundance	PBR	Trend	Classification
Gulf of Maine[*]	902	1.3	Increasing	Strategic
Eastern North Pacific	1,391[**]	2.3	Increasing	Strategic
Central North Pacific	4,005	12.9	Increasing	Strategic
Western North Pacific	394	1.3	Insufficient data	Strategic

[*]Most humpback whales in the North Atlantic are part of a single large population that breeds in the West Indies in winter and disperses to various feeding grounds, including the Gulf of Maine, in summer. Based on data from 1979 to 1993, Stevick et al. (2003) estimated the size of the "West Indies population" at 10,752 whales with an annual rate of increase at 3.1 percent.
[**]Calambokidis and Barlow (2004) estimate an abundance of 687 whales for the eastern North Pacific population.

North Atlantic right whale (*Eubalaena glacialis*) (ESA – endangered[5]; IUCN – endangered; MMPA – depleted)

Distribution and conservation units

Right whales occur in temperate to subtropical latitudes in both the Northern and Southern Hemispheres. The initial Recovery Plan for the Northern Right Whale treated all Northern Hemisphere right whales as a single species with two populations (NMFS 1991b). However, the current convention is to recognize the North Atlantic right whale (*E. glacialis*) and North Pacific right whale (*E. japonica*) as separate species (Rosenbaum et al. 2000). The revised recovery plan dealt only with *E. glacialis* (NMFS 2005), and NMFS is currently taking steps to recognize current right whale taxonomy in ESA listings (68 Fed. Reg. 17560). Western North Atlantic right whales feed between spring and fall in waters off New England and southeastern Canada. In fall, reproductive females and some juveniles migrate to winter calving grounds primarily off Georgia and Florida (Perry et al. 1999). Five major concentration areas have been identified in coastal waters off the United States and Canada including the nearshore waters of Florida and Georgia, the Great South Channel, Cape Cod Bay, the Bay of Fundy, and the Scotian Shelf.

History of evaluation and listing

The right whale is under the jurisdiction of NMFS. Milestones relative to the species' listing include the following:

- Species listed as endangered under the ESCA in 1970.
- Endangered status carried forward under the ESA in 1973.
- Qualified as depleted under the MMPA in 1973 by virtue of its listing under the ESA.
- Recovery plan adopted in 1991.

---

[5] Right whales are currently listed under the ESA as a single species, but here we consider whales in the North Atlantic and North Pacific as separate taxa. This is consistent with currently accepted taxonomy and also reflects the fact that NMFS is in the process of making regulatory changes to list them separately (68 Fed. Reg. 17560).

- Listed as endangered by the IUCN in 1996.
- Revised recovery plan adopted in 2005.

No detailed explanation was given when the right whale was listed as endangered under the ESCA in 1970 (35 Fed. Reg. 18319). Because the species was already listed when the ESA was passed in 1973, a formal analysis of threats and ESA listing factors was not done at that time.

The most recent ESA status review of right whales was published in 1999 (Perry et al. 1999). The review states, "Any reevaluation of northern and southern right whale status awaits collection of more reliable information on abundance, distribution, and threats from human activities…as well as the development of objective delisting criteria." It makes no specific recommendation for reclassifying or delisting the species under the ESA. ESA listing factors identified in the status review as possibly influencing recovery were destruction or modification of habitat (offshore oil and gas development, pollution, and channel dredging); overutilization (whale-watching and scientific research), regulatory inadequacy (a lack of vessel traffic and fishing regulations); and other factors (vessel collisions and entanglement in fishing gear).

The 2005 revised Recovery Plan for the North Atlantic Right Whale states, "There has been no apparent sign of recovery in the previous 15 years and the species may be rarer and more endangered than previously thought." It goes on to state, "The possibility of biological extinction in the next century is very real." The plan states that its ultimate goal is "to promote the recovery of North Atlantic right whales to a level sufficient to warrant their removal from the List of Endangered and Threatened Wildlife and Plants under the ESA," and its intermediate goal is "to reclassify the species from endangered to threatened" (NMFS 2005). Criteria for reclassification from endangered to threatened were specified in the plan as follows:

- All available data indicate that the population is increasing.
- The population has increased for a period of 35 years at an average rate of at least 2 percent per year.
- None of the ESA listing factors are known to be limiting population growth.
- A peer-reviewed population viability analysis shows that the population has no more than a 1 percent chance of reaching the quasi-extinction level in 100 years.

Criteria for delisting North Atlantic right whales were not included in the recovery plan because NMFS concluded that decades of population growth would need to occur before delisting could be considered.

The 2005 recovery plan includes an analysis of the five ESA listing factors that concluded as follows:

A. *The present or threatened destruction, modification, or curtailment of its habitat or range*—Habitat degradation may occur from a number of sources (e.g., oil spills, vessel traffic, noise, dredging, and contaminants) and actions should be taken to ensure that habitats are protected.

B. *Overutilization for commercial, recreational, scientific, or educational purposes*—Recreational, scientific, and educational activities are regulated, and currently no whales may be taken for commercial purposes. Prior to delisting, it should be affirmed that such activities will be adequately regulated in the future.

C. *Disease or predation*—No evidence indicates that these factors are limiting recovery, but few data are available. Prior to delisting, it should be affirmed that disease is not affecting the population and is not likely to do so in the foreseeable future.

D. *The inadequacy of existing regulatory mechanisms*—Regulations may be insufficient to adequately protect the population. In particular, it may be necessary to strengthen regulations to eliminate or reduce ship strikes and entanglement in fishing gear.

E. *Other natural or manmade factors affecting its continued existence*—No natural factors are known to be limiting recovery. Human factors known to be of high significance are ship strikes and entanglement in fishing gear. Other human factors of concern include contaminants, coastal development, and noise.

In 1996 the IUCN listed the North Atlantic right whale as endangered based on criterion D1 (IUCN 1996). The status of North Atlantic right whales was most recently evaluated by the IUCN Cetacean Specialist Group in 2003 (Reeves et al. 2003). Ship strikes and entanglement in fishing gear were identified as the most significant threats in that review.

North Atlantic right whales are considered as depleted under the MMPA because of their ESA listing. Their status relative to OSP has not been evaluated.

Available data

Prior to the listing of northern right whales under the ESCA in 1970, information on North Atlantic right whales was limited to historical whaling records and reports of scattered opportunistic sightings. In the late 1970s and early 1980s, a dedicated research program was developed through the efforts of independent scientists. Research since then has made this species one of the most extensively studied large whale species in the world. Most research has been carried out by non-governmental scientists with funding from federal agencies. NMFS provides the principal source of funding, although the U.S. Navy, Coast Guard, Army Corps of Engineers, various state agencies, and non-governmental foundations and groups also provide significant contributions.

The central pillar of available data is a photo-identification catalogue believed to include most of the population. The catalogue includes information on the age (year born or first sighted) and sex for a large proportion of the current population. Extensive aerial and shipboard sighting surveys provide resighting information from which life history information (e.g., calving rates, movement patterns, survival and mortality rates, injury and entanglement rates, etc.) can be derived. Genetic samples have been collected from many known individuals to assess filial relationships and confirm individual identifications. A dedicated carcass salvage program expanded in the early 1990s provides information on causes of many deaths.

A population model has been developed for the North Atlantic right whale population (Caswell et al. 1999) that has been used for population viability analysis.

Current biological status

Commercial hunting of right whales began as early as the 11th century in the eastern North Atlantic, in the 1500s off eastern Canada, and in the 1600s along the East Coast of the United States (Reeves 2001); there are no estimates of pre-exploitation population size (NMFS 1991b, Perry et al. 1999) although catch records indicate the population numbered at least a few thousand (Reeves 2001). The North Atlantic population may have numbered fewer than 100 animals when international protection was put in place in 1935. NMFS published the most recent SAR for North Atlantic right whales in 2005 (see http://www.nmfs.noaa.gov/pr/sars/species.htm), and estimated the population size in 1998 as 299. There is some indication that the population grew slowly during 1986–1992, but the survival rate declined in the 1990s. The SAR states that because of the likelihood that the population is declining the PBR is set at 0 animals. It also states that North Atlantic right whales are a strategic stock because they are listed as endangered under the ESA and because average annual fishery mortality and serious injury exceed PBR.

Caswell et al. (1999) have estimated that the North Atlantic right whales began declining at 2.4 percent per year in the 1990s. They predict that, if current conditions continue, the upper bound on expected time to extinction is 191 years.

North Pacific right whale (*Eubalaena japonica*) (ESA – endangered[6]; IUCN – endangered; MMPA – depleted)

Distribution and conservation units

Right whales occur in temperate to subtropical latitudes in both hemispheres. The initial Recovery Plan for the Northern Right Whale treated all Northern Hemisphere right whales as a single species with two populations (NMFS 1991b). However, North Pacific right whales (*E. japonica*) are currently considered a species distinct from the North Atlantic (*E. glacialis*; Rosenbaum et al. 2000). The revised recovery plan dealt only with *E. glacialis* (NMFS 2005), and NMFS is currently taking steps to recognize current right whale taxonomy in ESA listings (68 Fed. Reg. 17560). In the North Pacific right whales were once found throughout the ocean basin north of 35 degrees (Clapham et al. 2004, Shelden et al. 2005). They now occur in separate groups in the east and west that presumably constitute separate populations (Perry et al. 1999, Clapham et al. 2004).

History of evaluation and listing

The right whale is under the jurisdiction of NMFS. Milestones relative to the species' listing include the following:

---

[6] See note 5 above.

- Species listed as endangered under the ESCA in 1970.
- Endangered status carried forward under the ESA in 1973.
- Qualified as depleted under the MMPA in 1973 by virtue of its listing under the ESA.
- Recovery plan published in 1991.
- Listed as endangered by the IUCN in 1996.

No detailed explanation was given when the right whale was listed as endangered under the ESCA in 1970 (35 Fed. Reg. 18319). Because the species was already listed when the ESA was passed in 1973, a formal analysis of threats and ESA listing factors was not done at that time.

The 1991 Recovery Plan for the Northern Right Whale devotes most of its attention to the western Atlantic population. With regard to the eastern Pacific population, the plan notes that at the time it was written there were no predictable areas where right whales occurred and therefore it was impossible to propose specific recovery measures (NMFS 1991b). The plan did not identify any major threats for the eastern Pacific stock, but they were assumed to be similar to those for the western Atlantic population (i.e., vessel interactions, entanglement in fishing gear, and habitat degradation).

The most recent ESA status review of right whales was published in 1999 (Perry et al. 1999). It states, "The eastern North Pacific right whale stock remains severely depleted. Virtually nothing is known about its current size, trends in abundance, distribution, or migration patterns. The size of this stock is thought to be very small, but there are no reliable estimates of abundance. The classification of this stock should not change at this time, and is not likely to change in the foreseeable future." ESA listing factors identified in the status review as possibly influencing recovery were destruction or modification of habitat (offshore oil and gas development) and other factors (entanglement in fishing gear).

In 1996 the IUCN listed the North Pacific right whale as endangered based on criterion D1 (IUCN 1996). The status of North Pacific right whales was most recently evaluated by the IUCN Cetacean Specialist Group in 2003 (Reeves et al. 2003). Ship strikes and entanglement in fishing gear were identified as the most significant threats.

North Pacific right whales are considered as depleted under the MMPA because of their ESA listing. Their status relative to OSP has not been evaluated.

Available data

Prior to listing under the ESCA in 1970, information on right whales in the eastern North Pacific was limited almost entirely to historical whaling records and reports of scattered opportunistic sightings. From 1970 to the mid-1990s information was limited to rare opportunistic sighting records scattered in the region from Southern California to Alaska to Hawaii. No dedicated studies were possible because there was no location in the eastern North Pacific where right whales were known to occur regularly in any numbers. Since 1997 when a small group of right whales was found in the southeastern Bering Sea, efforts have been undertaken each summer in that area to locate, photograph, and collect biopsy samples from individuals. With almost no recent information on their occurrence in other areas or during other seasons, eastern North Pacific right whales are the least well known of all listed marine mammals in U.S. waters.

No models designed specifically for population viability analysis have been developed for North Pacific right whales.

<u>Current biological status</u>

Commercial hunting of right whales in the western North Pacific began in the 1500s along the Asian coast; there are no estimates of their pre-exploitation abundance (Perry et al. 1999). In the mid- to late 1800s intensive whaling occurred in the eastern North Pacific and by the end of the 19th century, right whales were rare throughout the region. The most recent SAR for North Pacific right whales was published in 2003 (see http://www.nmfs.noaa.gov/pr/sars/species.htm). The SAR does not provide a population estimate but notes that a few right whales have been seen in a portion of the southeastern Bering Sea each summer since 1996 and a very few sightings have been made in other areas. As of 2005, 23 individuals had been identified by photo-identification or genetic samples collected between 1998 and 2004 (P. Wade, pers. comm.). The population size may be only a few tens of animals, and its trend is unknown. The SAR does not calculate a PBR because there are insufficient data to estimate population size. It states that North Pacific right whales are considered a strategic stock because they are listed as endangered under the ESA.

Sei whale (*Balaenoptera borealis*) (ESA – endangered; IUCN – endangered; MMPA – depleted)

<u>Distribution and conservation units</u>

The sei whale is a cosmopolitan species with separate subspecies in the Northern and Southern Hemispheres (Rice 1998). Animals found in the North Atlantic, North Pacific, and Southern Oceans are almost certainly separate populations and are dealt with separately in the draft Recovery Plan for the Fin Whale and Sei Whale (NMFS 1998b). For purposes of preparing SARs required by the MMPA, NMFS has identified three stocks—Nova Scotia (formerly called the western North Atlantic stock), eastern North Pacific, and Hawaii. Sei whales range widely in oceanic waters of the North Atlantic and North Pacific, migrating from high-latitude summer feeding areas to lower-latitude winter breeding areas.

<u>History of evaluation and listing</u>

The sei whale is under the jurisdiction of NMFS. Milestones relative to the species' listing include the following:

- Species listed as endangered under the ESCA in 1970.
- Endangered status carried forward under the ESA in 1973.
- Qualified as depleted under the MMPA in 1973 by virtue of its listing under the ESA.
- Listed as endangered by the IUCN in 1996.
- Draft recovery plan prepared in 1998 but not adopted.

No detailed explanation was given when the sei whale was listed as endangered under the ESCA in 1970 (35 Fed. Reg. 18319). Because the species was already listed when the ESA was passed in 1973, a formal analysis of threats and ESA listing factors was not done at that time.

A draft Recovery Plan for the Fin Whale and Sei Whale was prepared by NMFS, but no action has been taken to adopt it. The draft plan states that its goal is "to promote recovery of all fin and sei whale populations to levels at which it becomes appropriate to downlist them from endangered to threatened status, and ultimately to remove them from the list of Endangered and Threatened Wildlife and Plants, under the provisions of the ESA" (NMFS 1998b). The draft plan suggests that, because they rarely occur in nearshore waters, sei whales may be less susceptible to human-caused threats than fin whales.

The most recent review of the status of sei whales under the ESA was published in 1999 (Perry et al. 1999). It states, "Any reevaluation of sei whale status awaits the collection of more reliable information on stock structure, distribution and migration patterns, trends in abundance, causes of mortality, and factors influencing the recovery of sei whales stocks, as well as the development of objective delisting criteria." It makes no specific recommendation for reclassifying or delisting the species under the ESA. ESA listing factors identified in the status review as possibly influencing recovery were destruction or modification of habitat (offshore oil and gas development); overutilization (whale-watching, scientific research, photography, and associated vessel traffic; Icelandic harvests), disease (parasite infestations), and other factors (vessel collisions).

In 1996 the IUCN listed sei whales as endangered worldwide based on criteria A1a, A1b, and A1d (IUCN 1996). Individual populations were not evaluated separately. The status of sei whales was most recently evaluated by the IUCN Cetacean Specialist Group in 2003 (Reeves et al. 2003). No specific threats were identified in that review.

Sei whales are considered as depleted under the MMPA because of their ESA listing. Their status relative to OSP has not been evaluated.

Available data

Prior to listing under the ESCA in 1970, information on sei whales in U.S. waters was limited almost exclusively to data associated with efforts to manage commercial whaling (e.g., catch and sighting records and tag recovery). Since 1970 there has been no directed research program on sei whales in the United States, and available information is limited to a few isolated studies, sighting reports during aerial and shipboard surveys for other marine mammals, and stranding records. For populations in U.S. waters, information on abundance, population dynamics, and trends ranges from very limited to almost none.

No models designed specifically for population viability analysis have been developed for sei whale populations in U.S. waters.

<u>Current biological status</u>

Sei whale populations in both the North Atlantic and North Pacific Oceans were greatly reduced by commercial whaling during the early and mid-1900s (NMFS 1998b). The pre-exploitation population size for the entire North Pacific Ocean has been estimated at 42,000, but there is no comparable estimate for the North Atlantic Ocean (Perry et al. 1999). NMFS SARs for sei whales were published in 2003 for the eastern North Pacific stock and in 2005 for the Nova Scotia and Hawaii stocks (see http://www.nmfs.noaa.gov/pr/sars/species.htm). Stock status parameters given in the SARs are shown here.

Stock name	Abundance	PBR	Trend	Classification
Nova Scotia	No reliable estimate	Unknown	Insufficient data	Strategic
Eastern North Pacific	56	0.1	Insufficient data	Strategic
Hawaii	77	0.1	Insufficient data	Strategic

Sperm whale (*Physeter macrocephalus*) (ESA – endangered; IUCN – vulnerable; MMPA – depleted)

<u>Distribution and conservation units</u>

The sperm whale is a cosmopolitan species occurring in all the world's oceans except the Arctic Ocean; there are no recognized subspecies (Rice 1998). It is generally recognized, however, that there are a number of discrete populations. For purposes of preparing SARs required by the MMPA, NMFS has identified five stocks—North Atlantic, California-Oregon-Washington, North Pacific, Hawaii, and northern Gulf of Mexico. Sperm whales occur throughout deeper parts of the North Atlantic and North Pacific Oceans from the equator to polar regions. Mature females, calves, and immature animals stay in temperate and tropical waters while adult males range farther north.

<u>History of evaluation and listing</u>

The sperm whale is under the jurisdiction of NMFS. Milestones relative to the species' listing include the following:

- Species listed as endangered under the ESCA in 1970.
- Endangered status carried forward under the ESA in 1973.

- Qualified as depleted under the MMPA in 1973 by virtue of its listing under the ESA.
- Listed as vulnerable by the IUCN in 1996.
- Draft recovery plan released for public review in 2006.

No detailed explanation was given when the sperm whale was listed as endangered under the ESCA in 1970 (35 Fed. Reg. 18319). Because the species was already listed when the ESA was passed in 1973, a formal analysis of threats and ESA listing factors was not done at that time.

The most recent ESA status review of sperm whales was published in 1999 (Perry et al. 1999). It states, "Any reevaluation of sperm whale classification status awaits the collection of more reliable information on distribution, migration patterns, abundance, and trends in abundance on a stock-specific basis, as well as the development of objective delisting criteria." It also suggests that the North Atlantic and North Pacific populations might be candidates for downlisting if better information becomes available on their abundance and stock identity and if human-related sources of mortality are controlled. ESA listing factors identified in the status review as possibly influencing recovery were destruction or modification of habitat (pollution, and offshore oil and gas development); overutilization (whale-watching, scientific research, and associated vessel traffic); disease or predation (papillomavirus and calicivirus and killer whale predation), and other factors (entanglement in fishing gear).

In July 2006 NMFS released a draft Recovery Plan for the Sperm Whale for public review (71 Fed. Reg. 38385).

In 1996 the IUCN listed sperm whales worldwide as vulnerable based on criteria A1b and A1d (IUCN 1996). Individual populations were not evaluated separately. The status of sperm whales was most recently evaluated by the IUCN Cetacean Specialist Group in 2003 (Reeves et al. 2003). Ship strikes and entanglement in fishing gear were identified as potential threats at the time.

Sperm whales are considered as depleted under the MMPA because of their ESA listing. Their status relative to OSP has not been evaluated.

Available data

Prior to listing under the ESCA in 1970, information on sperm whales in U.S. waters was limited almost exclusively to data associated with efforts to manage commercial whaling (e.g., catch and sighting records and tag recovery). Since 1970 there has been no directed sperm whale research program in the United States, and available information is limited to a few isolated studies, sighting reports during aerial and shipboard surveys for other marine mammals, and stranding records. Probably the best known population in U.S. waters is in the Gulf of Mexico where the Minerals Management Service has recently supported studies to tag and track sperm whales to help assess impacts of noise from offshore oil and gas exploration and development. Very few directed studies have been undertaken on sperm whales in U.S. waters of the Atlantic or Pacific. For the populations in U.S. waters, information on abundance, population dynamics, and trends varies from very limited to almost none.

No models designed specifically for population viability analysis have been developed for sperm whale populations in U.S. waters.

Current biological status

Sperm whale populations in the North Atlantic and especially the North Pacific were heavily harvested by commercial whalers from the 1800s to the mid-1900s (Perry et al. 1999). Pre-exploitation abundance estimates for the North Pacific and North Atlantic are in the hundreds of thousands, but those estimates are considered unreliable (Perry et al. 1999). The most recent SARs for sperm whales were published in 2003 for the California-Oregon-Washington and northern Gulf of Mexico stocks and in 2005 for the North Atlantic, North Pacific, and Hawaii stocks (see http://www.nmfs.noaa.gov/pr/sars/species.htm). Stock status parameters given in the SARs are shown here.

Stock name	Abundance	PBR	Trend	Classification
North Atlantic	4,804	7.0	Insufficient data	Strategic
California-Oregon-Washington	1,233	1.8	Insufficient data	Strategic
North Pacific	No reliable estimate[*]	Unknown	Insufficient data	Strategic
Hawaii	7,082	11.0	Insufficient data	Strategic
Gulf of Mexico	1,349	2.2	Insufficient data	Strategic

[*]Barlow and Taylor (2005) estimated the number of sperm whales in a region of the eastern North Pacific extending from the West Coast of the United States to Hawaii as 26,300 based on visual surveys and 32,100 based on acoustic surveys. The surveys included all or part of the range of the California-Oregon-Washington, North Pacific, and Hawaii stocks.

Beluga whale, Cook Inlet population (*Delphinapterus leucas*) (ESA – not listed; IUCN – critically endangered; MMPA – depleted)

Distribution and conservation units

Beluga whales occur only in arctic and subarctic waters of the Northern Hemisphere and are considered a single species with no identified subspecies (Rice 1998). Genetics studies confirm five demographically isolated populations in Alaska that each have their own summer concentration areas (O'Corry-Crowe et al. 1997). For purposes of preparing SARs required by the MMPA, NMFS has identified five stocks, only one of which, the Cook Inlet population, has been listed. Cook Inlet beluga whales are isolated both genetically and geographically. They are separated from the nearest other beluga whale population in the Bering Sea by the 900-km-long Alaska Peninsula. Cook Inlet beluga whales currently occur mostly in Cook Inlet where they seem to remain throughout the year (Hobbs et al. 2005). In summer they are most common near the mouths of large rivers in the upper inlet. A small group occurs in Yakutat Bay where they may be resident. Few sightings have been made in adjacent waters of the Gulf of Alaska (NMFS in prep.[c]).

History of evaluation and listing

The Cook Inlet beluga whale is under the jurisdiction of NMFS. Milestones relative to the population's listing include the following:

- Population listed as a candidate species for listing under the ESA in 1988.
- Species listed as vulnerable by the IUCN in 1996.
- NMFS petitioned in 1999 to list Cook Inlet beluga whales as depleted under the MMPA and endangered under the ESA.
- Population listed as depleted under the MMPA in 2000.
- Determination made that ESA listing was not warranted in 2000.
- Draft conservation plan released for public review in 2005.
- Listed as critically endangered by the IUCN in 2006.

In 1998 NMFS initiated a status review for the Cook Inlet beluga whale population (63 Fed. Reg. 64228). Reasons given for initiating the review were that (1) beluga whale counts made in 1998 were the lowest on record and had been declining since at least 1994, and (2) Alaska Native subsistence harvests, which had risen from about 15 whales per year in the early 1990s to about 100 whales per year (including whales struck and lost) in the mid-1990s, appeared to be exceeding sustainable levels.

In 1999 NMFS received petitions from the State of Alaska to list Cook Inlet beluga whales as depleted under the MMPA and from several organizations and individuals to list them as endangered under the ESA (64 Fed. Reg. 17347). NMFS determined that each of the petitions presented substantial information indicating that the listing action might be warranted, and later in 1999 it published a proposed rule to designate the population as depleted (64 Fed. Reg. 65298). In 2000 NMFS listed the population as depleted (65 Fed. Reg. 34590), noting that the abundance estimate for 1998 (347 whales) was likely less than 35 percent of K (estimated to be at least 1,000), which would be far below the population's MNPL level. The notice did not directly address causes of the decline or threats to the population.

Later in 2000 NMFS determined that the Cook Inlet population did not merit listing as endangered or threatened under the ESA based on its conclusion that the population was not in danger of extinction or likely to become so in the foreseeable future (65 Fed. Reg. 38778). The notice acknowledged that the population was small and had declined markedly in recent years. With regard to ESA listing factors NMFS concluded the following:

A. *The present or threatened destruction, modification, or curtailment of its habitat or range*—"A significant part of the habitat for this species has been modified by municipal, industrial and recreational activities in Upper Cook Inlet. However, the data do not support a conclusion that the range of CI belugas has been diminished by these activities."

B. *Overutilization for commercial, recreational, scientific, or educational purposes*—Mortality caused by overharvesting by Alaska Natives is of serious concern, and some of the products resulting from those harvests have been sold.

C. *Disease or predation*—There is no indication that disease has been a significant factor in the decline. Killer whale predation does occur but is not likely to be having a significant impact.

D. *The inadequacy of existing regulatory mechanisms*—Although there is a need to regulate subsistence hunting and development in beluga whale habitats, "NMFS believes that an inadequate regulatory mechanism has not caused the stock to become in danger of extinction, nor is it likely to do so in the foreseeable future."

E. *Other natural or manmade factors affecting its continued existence*—A number of other factors were identified that could affect Cook Inlet beluga whales including stochastic events, strandings, subsistence harvests, fishery interactions, oil spills, other pollutants, noise, and prey availability. The only one of these factors that was thought to be of significance was subsistence harvesting.

Overall NMFS concluded that because "legislative and management actions have been taken to reduce the subsistence harvest to levels that will allow the beluga whale stock to recover," a listing under the ESA was not warranted. The decision was appealed by some of the petitioners but was upheld in federal appeals court.

In 2005 NMFS released a draft Conservation Plan for the Cook Inlet Beluga Whale for public review (70 Fed. Reg. 12853). Its stated goal is recovery of the Cook Inlet stock of beluga whales to a population size of no fewer than 780 whales (NMFS in prep.[c]). The plan reviews the population's biology and status, as well as natural and human factors that could be affecting its recovery. It also contains a section on ESA listing that analyzes the five ESA listing factors and concludes that "there is evidence that one or more of these factors would apply to this stock." It also notes that the decision in 2000 not to list the population was based on the assumption that subsistence hunting was the only factor affecting the population, and that, because the population has not grown as expected since hunting has been controlled, the assumption may have been wrong. It goes on to state, "In consideration of the factors described above, and because it has been five years since the last Status Review for these whales occurred, we believe it is appropriate to again assess this stock for possible listing under the ESA. Therefore, NMFS will initiate a formal Status Review for the CI beluga whale commensurate with the development of this Conservation Plan." In 2006 NMFS announced in the *Federal Register* that it was again initiating a review of the status of Cook Inlet beluga whales to determine whether they should be listed under the ESA (71 Fed. Reg. 14836).

In 1996 the IUCN listed the entire beluga whale species as vulnerable based on criteria A1a, A1b, and A1d (IUCN 1996). The Cook Inlet population was not evaluated separately. The status of beluga whales was evaluated by the IUCN Cetacean Specialist Group in 2003 (Reeves et al. 2003). General threats to the species identified in the review were hunting and vessel traffic. An assessment specific to the Cook Inlet population was conducted by the IUCN Cetacean Specialist Group in

2006 (Lowry et al. 2006), and the population was listed as critically endangered in the 2006 IUCN Red List.

Available data

Relatively little research has been done on Cook Inlet beluga whales. From the 1960s to the 1980s, a few counts were made by the ADFG and other biologists. In 1993 NMFS began flying beluga whale surveys in Cook Inlet. Based on those surveys, population estimates using standardized methods have been produced each year since 1994. Satellite telemetry studies also have been undertaken to track beluga whale movements, distribution, and behavior. Some data on genetics, contaminants, and life history have been collected from animals stranded and taken by Alaska Natives for subsistence purposes. It has generally been assumed that biological characteristics of Cook Inlet beluga whales are similar to those of western Alaska beluga whale populations that have been better studied.

A population model specific to Cook Inlet beluga whales that can be used for population viability analysis has been developed (D. Goodman, unpub.).

Current biological status

The most recent SAR for Cook Inlet beluga whales was published in 2005 (see http://www.nmfs .noaa.gov/pr/sars/species.htm). It gives a population estimate of 357 whales and calculates a PBR of 2.0 animals per year. The population size estimates declined rapidly from 1994 (653 animals) to 1998 (349 animals), after which the decline appeared to stop. Annual abundance estimates for 1999–2004 have ranged from 313 to 435 and show no trend (NMFS in prep.[c]). The estimate for 2005 was 278 (R. Hobbs, pers. comm.). An analysis of population growth that includes the 2005 count suggests that the population is most likely declining at about 1 percent per year (Lowry et al. 2006). The SAR states that Cook Inlet beluga whales are a strategic stock because they are listed as depleted under the MMPA. Identified sources of human-caused mortality are subsistence hunting and incidental take in fisheries, both of which appear to be very small at the current time.

Bottlenose dolphin, mid-Atlantic coastal population (*Tursiops truncatus*) (ESA – not listed; IUCN – data deficient; MMPA – depleted)

Distribution and conservation units

Bottlenose dolphins occur in tropical and temperate regions of the North Pacific and North Atlantic Oceans in both coastal and offshore waters. Although they are currently considered a single species with no identified subspecies, their taxonomy and population structure are not fully resolved (Rice 1998). It was previously thought that a single coastal migratory stock ranged along the U.S. Atlantic coast from as far north as Long Island, New York, to as far south as central Florida (Scott et al. 1988). It was this "mid-Atlantic" coastal population that was listed as depleted under the MMPA after a large dolphin die-off along the U.S. mid-Atlantic coast in the late 1980s. However, new information suggests that their stock structure is more complicated. For purposes of preparing SARs required by the MMPA, NMFS currently uses eight bottlenose dolphin management units along the U.S. Atlantic coast.

History of evaluation and listing

The mid-Atlantic coastal bottlenose dolphin is under the jurisdiction of NMFS. Milestones relative to the population's listing include the following:

- Petitioned to list the mid-Atlantic coastal population as depleted in 1988.
- Population listed as depleted under the MMPA in 1993.
- Listed as data deficient by the IUCN in 1996.

In 1987–1988 a major die-off of bottlenose dolphins occurred along the U.S. Atlantic coast. Shortly thereafter, NMFS estimated that the regional population could have been reduced by as much as 60 percent. As a result, the Center for Marine Conservation petitioned NMFS to list the population as depleted under the MMPA. Final action to do so was completed in 1993 (58 Fed. Reg. 17789). In its analysis of population status, NMFS was unable to compare pre- and post-die-off population sizes because of insufficient abundance data. Instead, it described a model that looked at estimates of stranding rates, natural mortality rates, and birth rates, and estimated that there had been a 53 percent reduction in abundance during the die-off period (54 Fed. Reg. 41654). Because this would have resulted in a population size less than 50 percent of its carrying capacity (assuming that carrying capacity had not changed) and thus below its OSP level, NMFS concluded that the population was depleted under the MMPA definition. Although the final rule advised that NMFS would prepare a conservation plan for the population, this was assigned a low priority relative to work on other listed species and work to develop a bottlenose dolphin take reduction plan. As a result, the conservation plan has not been completed.

In 1996 the IUCN listed the bottlenose dolphin as data deficient (IUCN 1996). The U.S. mid-Atlantic coastal population was not evaluated separately. The status of bottlenose dolphins was most recently evaluated by the IUCN Cetacean Specialist Group in 2003 (Reeves et al. 2003). Acute threats were identified in some regions but not for the western North Atlantic, although the report notes the occasional occurrence of major unexplained mortality events.

Available data

Prior to its listing as depleted in 1993, information on the Atlantic coastal migratory population of bottlenose dolphins was limited primarily to data from some stranded animals and to an estimate of abundance and distribution obtained during a series of marine mammal and sea turtle surveys funded by the Bureau of Land Management between 1979 and 1981. Since 1993 periodic aerial and vessel surveys have been carried out to assess abundance. Recent research has focused largely on genetic studies using biopsy samples to better resolve the population structure and range of the various bottlenose dolphin groups along the Atlantic coast. Determining the distribution and overlap in ranges between what appear to be separate coastal and offshore migratory populations is particularly important. Other recent research has included studies to track the movements of a few individual dolphins with satellite-linked tags and efforts to monitor causes of mortality of stranded animals. Overall, abundance, trends, population parameters, and other details of the Atlantic coastal migratory population remain poorly known, although significant studies have been done in some local areas (e.g., Read et al. 2003).

No models designed specifically for population viability analysis have been developed for bottlenose dolphins in U.S waters.

Current biological status

NMFS most recently revised the SAR for the mid-Atlantic coastal population of bottlenose dolphins (now called the western North Atlantic coastal population) in 2005 (see http://www.nmfs.noaa .gov/pr/sars/species.htm). Abundance estimates are given for a number of migratory and non-migratory components of the population and suggest a total abundance of about 33,000. Population trend is unknown. Rather than calculating a single PBR for the total population, the SAR calculates multiple PBRs for a complex of small management units. It states that the western North Atlantic coastal population is considered a strategic stock because it is listed as depleted under the MMPA and because incidental takes in fisheries exceed PBR in some areas. The SAR further notes that although the coastal migratory population is designated as depleted under the MMPA, the depletion designation should be reevaluated based on the current system of management units.

Killer whale, southern resident population (*Orcinus orca*) (ESA – endangered; IUCN – lower risk; MMPA – depleted)

Distribution and conservation units

The killer whale is currently considered a single species with no identified subspecies (Rice 1998). However, the current taxonomy is outdated and needs revision (Reeves et al. 2004, Krahn et al. 2004). Four populations of resident killer whales are recognized in the eastern North Pacific: southern, northern, southern Alaska, and western Alaska residents (Krahn et al. 2004). The southern resident population is the only listed taxon. Killer whales are locally common along the coast of the eastern North Pacific, especially from California northward. Southern residents are known to occur in the coastal waters off central California, Washington, Vancouver Island, and the Queen Charlotte Islands (Krahn et al. 2004).

History of evaluation and listing

The southern resident killer whale is under the jurisdiction of NMFS. Milestones relative to the population's listing include:

- Entire species listed as lower risk by the IUCN in 1996.
- NMFS petitioned to list the population as endangered or threatened under the ESA in 2001.
- NMFS determined that ESA listing was not warranted, but that MMPA listing may be warranted in 2002.
- Population listed as depleted under the MMPA in 2003.
- Finding relative to the ESA listing petition challenged in court, and NMFS directed to proceed with a listing proposal in 2003.
- Population listed as endangered under the ESA in 2005.

NMFS received a petition from the Center for Biological Diversity and several other organizations in 2001 to list the eastern North Pacific southern resident population of killer whales as an endangered or threatened species under the ESA. NMFS determined that the petition presented substantial information indicating that a listing may be warranted and thus conducted an ESA status review. A Biological Review Team (BRT) was established for this purpose and, in accordance with its report (Krahn et al. 2002), NMFS determined that southern resident killer whales are not a "species" as defined by the ESA and that listing was therefore not warranted (67 Fed. Reg. 44133). The BRT report identified potential risk factors that could influence the southern resident killer whale population, including changes in prey availability caused by fluctuations in environmental conditions, contaminants, noise from whale-watching vessels, diseases and parasites, declines in salmon stocks that are important prey, and catastrophes such as oil spills and harmful algal blooms.

Later in 2002 NMFS' decision was challenged in U.S. District Court. In 2003 the court set aside the not warranted finding, ruling that NMFS had erred in using incorrect taxonomy when determining whether southern resident killer whales constituted a distinct population segment under the ESA. The court therefore remanded the matter back to NMFS and required the agency to issue a new finding consistent with the court's order by December 2004. As a result a new BRT was convened to produce a new status report.

The 2004 status report (Krahn et al. 2004) concluded that North Pacific resident killer whales should be considered as an unnamed subspecies of the global killer whale species, and that the southern resident group likely comprises a distinct population segment of that subspecies. The report does not specifically address the five ESA listing factors but makes the following statements regarding threats to the population: "Concern remains about whether reduced quantity or quality of prey are affecting the Southern Resident population. In addition, levels of organochlorine contaminants are not declining appreciably and those of many newly emerging contaminants (e.g., brominated flame retardants) are increasing, so Southern Residents are likely at risk for serious chronic effects similar to those demonstrated for other marine mammal species (e.g., immune and reproductive system dysfunction). Other important risk factors that may continue to impact Southern Residents are oil spills and noise and disturbance from vessel traffic."

The report included a PVA model that predicted a 1 to 15 percent probability that the population would decline to a quasi-extinction threshold within 100 years and a 4 to 68 percent probability that it would do so within 300 years. The report also considered IUCN listing criteria and concluded that the taxon would qualify for listing under criterion D because it includes only 41 mature individuals. In conclusion, the report stated, "Taken together, the population dynamics of the Southern Residents describe a population that is at risk for extinction, due either to incremental small-scale impacts over time (e.g., reduced fecundity or subadult survivorship) or to a major catastrophe (e.g., disease outbreak or oil spill)." Based on findings of the status review, NMFS proposed listing southern resident killer whales as a threatened species under the ESA in 2004 (69 Fed. Reg. 76673).

In 2005 NMFS took final action to list the southern resident killer whale population as endangered under the ESA (70 Fed. Reg. 69903). The analysis of the five ESA listing factors accompanying the action concluded as follows:

A. *The present or threatened destruction, modification, or curtailment of its habitat or range*—The habitat of southern resident killer whales has been modified by contaminants, vessel traffic, and changes in prey availability.
B. *Overutilization for commercial, recreational, scientific, or educational purposes*—Capture for public display in the 1970s likely affected the southern resident killer whale population. Whale-watching may currently be having some impact.
C. *Disease or predation*—There is no evidence that disease has caused the population decline, but there is concern that high levels of contaminants may cause immunosuppression.
D. *The inadequacy of existing regulatory mechanisms*—Existing regulatory mechanisms have not been adequate to prevent contaminants from accumulating in southern resident killer whales.
E. *Other natural or manmade factors affecting its continued existence*—There is concern that an oil spill could impact the remaining population.

At the time NMFS initially declined to list southern resident killer whales under the ESA, scientific information evaluated during the status review (Krahn et al. 2002) indicated that the population might qualify as depleted under the MMPA. Therefore, in 2002 NMFS began the process for determining if the stock was depleted. In 2003 it determined that the taxon constituted a population stock as defined under the MMPA and that its abundance (80 animals in 2002) was below the lower bound of MNPL (84 based on an estimated minimum historical abundance of 140). Southern resident killer whales were therefore designated as depleted (68 Fed. Reg. 31980).

In its 1996 Red Book, the IUCN listed killer whales as lower-risk, conservation-dependent[7] (IUCN 1996). The southern resident population was not evaluated separately. The status of killer whales was most recently evaluated by the IUCN Cetacean Specialist Group in 2003 (Reeves et al. 2003). Threats to killer whales in the Washington–British Columbia region identified during that review were contaminants, depletion of prey populations, and disturbance from vessel traffic.

---

[7] See note 3 above.

The southern resident killer whale population has been well studied. Because killer whales can be identified from photographs and the southern resident population lives in an area easily accessed by scientists and whale-watchers, extensive population data have been collected annually. Most of its members are known individually and have been monitored over the past several decades or since birth. Most research on southern resident killer whales has been carried out by non-governmental scientists with funding from various foundations and other non-governmental sources in addition to NMFS. Distribution, abundance, movements, behavior, and life history parameters have been described in detail. Biopsy samples and stranded animals have provided data on genetics and contaminant levels.

In its 2004 status report (Krahn et al. 2004) the BRT for southern resident killer whales developed a population model and did a population viability analysis.

Current biological status

The most recent SAR for the southern resident population of killer whale, published in 2005 (see http://www.nmfs.noaa.gov/pr/sars/species.htm), reports a population size of 84 animals and states that the population has declined from 99 animals in 1995. It calculates a PBR of 0.8 and states that southern resident killer whales are a strategic stock because they are listed as depleted under the MMPA.

Killer whale, AT1 group (*Orcinus orca*) (ESA – not listed; IUCN – lower risk; MMPA – depleted)

Distribution and conservation units

Killer whales are currently considered a single species with no identified subspecies (Rice 1998). However, the current taxonomy is outdated and in need of revision (Reeves et al. 2004, Krahn et al. 2004). For purposes of preparing SARs required by the MMPA, NMFS recognizes seven killer whale stocks in U.S. waters. The AT1 group is considered to be part of the eastern North Pacific transient stock. Killer whales are common along the coast of the eastern North Pacific, especially from California northward. AT1 killer whales seem to have a very restricted distribution in the central Gulf of Alaska, occurring mostly in Prince William Sound and nearby fiords of the Kenai Peninsula.[8]

---

[8] http://www.fakr.noaa.gov/protectedresources/whales/killerwhales/at1statreview0703.pdf

History of evaluation and listing

The AT1 group of eastern North Pacific transient killer whales is under the jurisdiction of NMFS. Milestones relative to the taxon's listing include the following:

- Entire species listed as lower risk by the IUCN in 1996.
- NMFS petitioned to list the taxon as depleted under the MMPA in 2002.
- Taxon listed as depleted under the MMPA in 2004.

In 2002 NMFS was petitioned by the National Wildlife Federation and several other conservation groups to list AT1 killer whales as depleted under the MMPA. A status review in 2003 reported that the abundance of the AT1 group had declined from 22 animals in 1988 to 9 in 2002.[9] It also concluded that the AT1 group is "a genetically distinct, socially isolated group of killer whales" and that, while it is currently considered part of the eastern North Pacific transient stock, it probably qualifies as an independent population stock under the MMPA. The review goes on to state, "If the AT1 group is considered a population stock under the MMPA, there is little doubt that it would be considered to be below its MNPL level, as it has declined by more than 50 percent from historic levels (since 1984). Therefore, under that scenario, the AT1 group would be considered to be below OSP." Based on the status review, NMFS determined that the AT1 group is a population stock as defined by the MMPA and, therefore, designated the group as depleted in 2004 (69 Fed. Reg. 21321). Threats to the population identified in the status review were oil spills and other contaminants, declines in prey availability, fisheries interactions, and whale-watching and vessel traffic.

In its 1996 Red Book, the IUCN listed killer whales worldwide as lower-risk, conservation-dependent (IUCN 1996).[10] The AT1 group was not evaluated separately. The status of killer whales was most recently evaluated by the IUCN Cetacean Specialist Group in 2003 (Reeves et al. 2003), but the AT1 group was not specifically addressed.

Available data

The AT1 group of killer whales has been relatively well studied. Studies began in the late 1970s and intensified after the 1989 *Exxon Valdez* oil spill in Prince William Sound. Because killer whales can be identified from photographs, a considerable amount of data is available on the distribution, movements, and biological characteristics of individual members in the AT1 group. Biopsy samples and stranded animals have provided data on genetic relationships and contaminant levels.

No models designed specifically for population viability analysis have been developed for AT1 killer whales.

---

[9] Ibid.
[10] See note 3 above.

Current biological status

The most recent SAR for the AT1 group of transient killer whales, published in 2005 (see http://www.nmfs.noaa.gov/pr/sars/species.htm), reports a population size of eight animals and calculates a PBR level of zero. The trend in abundance is declining, and there have been no documented births since 1984. The SAR states that the AT1 killer whale group is a strategic stock because they are listed as depleted under the MMPA.

IV.   SUMMARY AND CONCLUSIONS

Characteristics of ESA, MMPA, and IUCN classification systems

The ESA is the principal U.S. law that requires actions to prevent extinction of species. It provides for the listing of species, subspecies, or distinct population segments as endangered or threatened based on their likelihood of going extinct within the foreseeable future. Species so listed are then eligible for protective provisions set forth in the Act. There is no set formula for making ESA listing determinations; rather they are based on an analysis of factors that may cause extinction.

Evaluation of marine mammals for listing under the ESA is done by either FWS (for sirenians, otters, walruses, and polar bears) or NMFS (all other species). For listing actions, FWS stresses an evaluation of threats using case-by-case professional judgment (DeMaster et al. 2004). Taxa are listed if one or more of the threat factors indicate a likelihood of extinction. Taxa may be reclassified or delisted based on a combination of population size, population trend, distribution, and abatement of threats (D. Crouse, pers. comm.). NMFS also considers the five factors when evaluating taxa for listing but recently has been giving more emphasis to use of "structured expert opinion" that looks at a variety of qualitative and quantitative measures of extinction risk, as well as an analysis of threats under the five listing factors (Angliss et al. 2002, DeMaster et al. 2004, M. Nammack, pers. comm.).

All marine mammals listed under the ESA are considered to be depleted under MMPA provisions. The MMPA also allows species or population stocks not listed under the ESA to be listed as depleted if they are determined to be below their OSP level. OSP is defined based on population size and population dynamics and is generally considered to be a range from the largest supportable in an ecosystem (K) down to the level at which the population shows maximum net productivity (generally considered to be 60 percent of K). Therefore, in addition to those taxa threatened with extinction, taxa listed as depleted may include some that are still quite abundant but are known to be substantially depleted compared to historical levels.

The IUCN listing system uses eight categories ranging from data deficient up to critically endangered. A combination of quantitative and qualitative criteria are used to assign taxa to the various categories. Although this approach has the advantage that criteria and thresholds for listing are specified, concern has been expressed that the IUCN system may not be optimal for marine mammals because it is intended primarily to evaluate species risk at the global level and is designed for all species, most of which have life history characteristics that are much different from those of cetaceans and pinnipeds (Angliss et al. 2002).

The ESA and IUCN systems have a similar purpose, that is to identify taxa at risk of becoming extinct within the foreseeable future. The comparability of the categories used by the two classification systems has not been formally analyzed, but the IUCN categories of critically endangered and endangered are roughly equivalent to ESA endangered, while the IUCN category vulnerable is similar to ESA threatened (Angliss et al. 2002). The MMPA category of depleted has no real biological equivalent in either the ESA or IUCN systems and, in some respects, is more similar to the category "overfished" under the Magnuson-Stevens Fisheries Conservation and Management Act. Nevertheless, the protections provided by the MMPA for depleted stocks are similar to the prohibitions on take of listed species under ESA.

A critical issue in listing is the taxonomic or population unit selected for evaluation. This is a subject where science and management are progressing rapidly, and it has become evident that in many cases proper conservation must address population units smaller than entire species (Taylor 2005). The current version of the ESA specifically recognizes the possible need to list distinct population segments, and federal agencies have specified policies for determining when such segments occur based on reproductive isolation and evolutionary considerations. However, many species were first listed in 1970 after the ESCA was passed and they have not been subjected to rigorous status reviews using more appropriate population units. The MMPA allows depleted designation for species or population stocks, the latter of which has a definition similar to that of a distinct population segment. The IUCN states that its primary purpose is evaluating species at the global level, but its listing system also allows for evaluations of lower taxonomic units and smaller geographic regions (IUCN 2004). Although all three systems allow for listings based on relevant conservation units, many listings are still for entire species worldwide.

The 1994 amendments to the MMPA require that NMFS and FWS prepare SARs for all stocks of marine mammals under their jurisdictions. The amendments further require that the agencies review the SARs annually for any stock designated as "strategic," which includes any taxon listed as endangered or threatened under the ESA or depleted under the MMPA. Therefore, the stocks referred to in the SARs should reflect the most current understanding of proper population units to use in conserving marine mammals based on the most recent scientific information. Table 3 shows, for selected large whale species, the population units used to make status evaluations in the ESA, IUCN, and MMPA SAR systems. For blue, fin, humpback, sei, and sperm whales, the ESA lists the entire species while the SARs provide separate evaluations of three to five stocks within each species. Clearly, for these species, currently available data and analyses show that status should be evaluated based on much smaller units than are currently used as the basis for ESA and IUCN classifications. The failure to use appropriate units very likely will result in both over-protection (e.g., a stock being considered as endangered as part of a global taxon when in fact the stock itself has recovered) and under-protection (e.g., a stock at risk not remaining listed as endangered or threatened because the global taxon has recovered). A reevaluation of the ESA listing status of large whales using currently accepted population units should be a high priority for action by NMFS.

Summary of species listing status

The 22 listed marine mammals include two sirenian populations, two sea otter populations, two phocid seal species, four otariid populations, eight species of large whales, and four populations of small whales or dolphins (Table 2). Under the ESA, 14 of these taxa are listed as endangered, 4 as threatened, and 4 are not listed. Eleven of the ESA listed taxa were first listed under the ESPA or ESCA, and six were listed subsequent to passage of the ESA. Of the four taxa not listed under the ESA, one was evaluated for listing and rejected, and three have not been evaluated. All 22 taxa are listed as depleted under the MMPA, 16 by virtue of their ESA listing and 6 as a result of a formal determination that their population was below OSP. The IUCN lists 1 of the taxa as extinct, 1 as critically endangered, 10 as endangered, 6 as vulnerable, and 4 as lower risk or data deficient.

Despite different criteria and methods used for status evaluations, the ESA and IUCN systems have resulted in quite comparable listings of most marine mammals. Fifteen of the 18 taxa listed as endangered or threatened under the ESA also are listed as critically endangered, endangered, or vulnerable by IUCN. Of the four taxa not listed under the ESA, one is listed as critically endangered by IUCN, and one is listed as vulnerable worldwide.

Some of the apparent discrepancies in how individual taxa are listed under the various systems are due to differing definitions of the listing categories. For example, a species can qualify as depleted under the MMPA because it is below OSP while it is still relatively numerous and not in immediate danger of extinction. The ESA and IUCN allow for use of different listing criteria, and therefore it is not surprising that taxa are sometimes assigned to slightly different categories under the two systems. Furthermore there are major differences in the nature of population units being evaluated for listing. The IUCN listings considered here generally applied to entire species worldwide, while recent ESA and MMPA listing actions have dealt more with population segments or stocks. Unless the population units being evaluated are identical, there is no reason to expect that different listing systems will produce comparable results.

Biological status of listed taxa

Most of the listed marine mammal taxa are not abundant, are known to be declining or of unknown trend, and are substantially reduced in numbers compared to historical levels (Table 4). However, there are some major variations. Estimates of abundance for taxa listed as endangered under the ESA range from 0 to 38,513, with only four taxa estimated to number more than 10,000. (Note, however, that abundance data are incomplete for several large whale taxa, and the numbers given are therefore underestimates.) Estimates for threatened taxa range from 2,825 to 44,996, with two numbering fewer than 10,000 and two more than 40,000. Abundance estimates for taxa listed as depleted under the MMPA but not listed under the ESA range from 8 to 688,028. Populations of two of those taxa are estimated to number fewer than 300 individuals. Of taxa listed as endangered under the ESA, five are known or thought to be increasing and three to be declining. (Note that large whales were considered increasing if any stock was increasing, but such a judgment is uncertain, given available data.) For threatened taxa, three are known or thought to be increasing and one declining. For taxa listed only as depleted, three are known or thought to be declining.

Species for which new information may warrant a reexamination of listing classifications

The quality of data currently available on the biology of listed species was subjectively evaluated based on expert judgment of the authors of this report in consultation with other species experts. Six general categories of population and ecological data were evaluated (Table 5). For only five taxa was data availability ranked as good in four or more of the six data categories considered. If both good and fair data quality are considered, the situation is much better—11 taxa have good or fair in all 6 categories and 2 have good or fair in 5 categories. At the other extreme, four taxa have poor data availability in all of the categories and eight in three or more categories.

Table 6 summarizes the biological and listing status for the 13 taxa that have good or fair data quality in at least five data categories. Although an evaluation of the appropriateness of current listing classifications was not the primary objective of this report, the table shows some obvious instances where reconsideration of listing status would appear to be appropriate. For example, western Arctic bowhead whales are relatively numerous and have been increasing steadily in abundance for at least the last 20 years. Consideration might be given to downlisting or delisting this population under ESA provisions. At least some stocks of humpback whales are both relatively numerous and increasing; these also might be candidates for downlisting or delisting if they are evaluated as appropriate distinct population segments using the most recent abundance data (e.g., from the SPLASH program). The eastern population of Steller sea lions is currently numerous and increasing and should be considered for ESA delisting. The western population of Steller sea lions is comparatively numerous and, if the apparent recent increasing trend is confirmed and continues long enough to convincingly be interpreted as more than just the effect of temporary environmental variation, the population might be considered for ESA downlisting. Two taxa listed as depleted under the MMPA but not currently listed under the ESA—AT1 killer whales and Cook Inlet beluga whales—are at very low population sizes and are not known to be recovering, and their ESA status should be reevaluated. Finally, the Caribbean monk seal, which has not been observed since the early 1950s, probably warrants delisting on grounds that it is now extinct.

Finally, it is important to remember that this review included only those taxa that are already listed under the MMPA and/or ESA and that our suggestions above deal only with a subset of those for which there are relatively good population data. There is legitimate concern among some marine mammal scientists that some other taxa may qualify for protective listing, and might in fact be among the "most endangered marine mammal populations" if adequate data were available to make an evaluation. However for those taxa we often do not know what the population units are that should be of conservation concern, what their historical and current abundances were and are, whether numbers are currently increasing or decreasing, and what factors may be threatening the population. Without such data, it is essentially impossible to conduct thorough status reviews or to compare population status with the listing criteria used by any system. In the absence of status reviews and listing evaluations, such taxa are *de facto* considered to be not endangered or threatened and not depleted and thus will not be afforded the extra protection that might be warranted. A good example of this are the various species of beaked whales. A more robust decision system is needed for coping with the likelihood that some species for which there is little available data are nevertheless endangered and in need of conservation attention. Evaluation of whether, and if so how, such taxa should be listed under the ESA and MMPA will be a huge challenge, but it is one that must be faced if the conservation and recovery goals of these laws are to be realized.

V. ACKNOWLEDGMENTS

A number of experts reviewed and commented on parts of this report, and for their efforts the authors thank Michael Payne, Michael Gosliner, John Reynolds, Deborah Crouse, Gregory Sanders, James Valade, Dawn Jennings, Diane Bowen, Melissa Andersen, and Jorge Saliva. We especially thank Randall Reeves, Daniel Goodman, and Suzanne Montgomery for their thorough and helpful reviews of the complete report. Preparation of this report was funded by the U.S. Marine Mammal Commission as part of a special project requested by the U.S. Congress.

VI. LITERATURE CITED

Angliss, R. P., G. K. Silber, and R. Merrick. 2002. Report of a workshop on developing recovery criteria for large whale species. NOAA Tech. Memo. NMFS-OPR-21. 32 pp.

Barlow, J., and B. L. Taylor. 2005. Estimates of sperm whale abundance in the northeastern temperate Pacific from a combined acoustic and visual survey. Marine Mammal Science 21:429–445.

Boyd, I. L., and M. P. Standford. 1998. Circumstantial evidence for the presence of monk seals in the West Indies. Oryx 32:310–316.

Burn, D. M., and A. M. Doroff. 2005. Decline in sea otter (*Enhydra lutris*) populations along the Alaska Peninsula, 1986–2001. Fishery Bulletin 103:270–279.

Calambokidis, J., and J. Barlow. 2004. Abundance of blue and humpback whales in the eastern North Pacific estimated by capture-recapture and line-transect methods. Marine Mammal Science 20:65–85.

Caswell, H., M. Fujiwara, and S. Brault. 1999. Declining survival probability threatens the North Atlantic right whale. Proceedings of the National Academy of Sciences 96:3308–3313.

Clapham, P. J., C. Good, S. E. Quinn, R. R. Reeves, J. E. Scarff, and R. L. Brownell, Jr. 2004. Distribution of North Pacific right whales (*Eubalaena japonica*) as shown by 19th and 20th century whaling catch and sighting records. Journal of Cetacean Research and Management 6:1–6.

Cronin, M. A., J. Bodkin, B. Bellachey, J. A. Estes, and J. C. Patton. 1996. Mitochondrial-DNA variation among subspecies and populations of sea otters (*Enhydra lutris*). Journal of Mammalogy 77:546–547.

DeMaster, D., R. Angliss, J. Cochrane, P. Mace, R. Merrick, M. Miller, S. Rumsey, B. Taylor, G. Thompson, and R. Waples. 2004. Recommendations to NOAA Fisheries: ESA Listing Criteria by the Quantitative Working Group, 10 June 2004. NOAA Tech. Memo. NMFSF/SPO-67. 85 pp.

Domning, D. P., and L. C. Hayek. 1986. Interspecific and intraspecific morphological variation in manatees (Sirenia: *Trichechus*). Marine Mammal Science 2:87–144.

Estes, J. A. 1990. Growth and equilibrium in sea otter populations. Journal of Animal Ecology 59:385–401.

Estes, J. A., M. T. Tinker, T. M. Williams, and D. F. Doak. 1998. Killer whale predation on sea otters linking oceanic and nearshore ecosystems. Science 282:473–476.

FWS. 1980. West Indian manatee recovery plan. U.S. Fish and Wildlife Service. Atlanta, GA. 27 pp.

FWS. 1986. Recovery Plan for the Puerto Rico Population of the West Indian (Antillean) Manatee (*Trichechus manatus manatus* L.). U.S. Fish and Wildlife Service. Atlanta, GA. 28 pp.

FWS. 2001. Florida Manatee Recovery Plan, (*Trichechus manatus latirostris*), Third Revision. U.S. Fish and Wildlife Service. Atlanta, GA. 144 pp. + appendices.

FWS. 2003. Final Revised Recovery Plan for the Southern Sea Otter (*Enhydra lutris nereis*). U.S. Fish and Wildlife Service. Portland, OR. 165 pp.

Gambell, R. 1976. World whale stocks. Mammal Review 6(1):41–53.

Gerber, L. R., and D. P. DeMaster. 1997. Endangered Species Act classification criteria for North Pacific humpback whales. Pages 203–211 *in* Marine Mammal Protection Act and Endangered Species Act Implementation Program 1996. NOAA NMFS AFSC Processed Rep. 97–10.

Gerber, L. R., and D. P. DeMaster. 1999. A quantitative approach to Endangered Species Act classification of long-lived vertebrates: application to the North Pacific humpback whale. Conservation Biology 13:1–12.

Gilmartin. W. G. 1983. Recovery plan for the Hawaiian monk seal, *Monachus schauinslandi*. NOAA, NMFS Tech. Rep. 29 pp. + tables, appendix.

Gorbics, C. S., and J. L. Bodkin. 2001. Stock structure of sea otters (*Enhydra lutris kenyoni*) in Alaska. Marine Mammal Science 17:632–647.

Hanni, K. D., D. J. Long, R .E. Jones, P. Pyle, and L. E. Morgan. 1997. Sightings and strandings of Guadalupe fur seals in central and northern California, 1988–1995. Journal of Mammalogy. 78:684–690.

Harting, A. L. 2002. Stochastic simulation model for the Hawaiian monk seal. Ph.D. thesis, Montana State University, Bozeman. 328 pp.

Haubold, E. M, C. Deutsch, and C. Fonnesbeck. 2005. Preliminary biological status review of the Florida manatee (*Trichechus manatus latirostris*). Florida Fish and Wildlife Conservation Commission, Fish and Wildlife Research Institute. St. Petersburg, FL.

Hobbs, R. C., K. L. Laidre, D. J. Vos, B. A Mahoney, and M. Eagleton. 2005. Movements and area use of belugas, *Delphinapterus leucas*, in a subarctic Alaskan estuary. Arctic 58:331–340.

IUCN. 1996. 1996 IUCN Red List of Threatened Animals. IUCN, Gland, Switzerland. 70 + 368 pp.

IUCN. 2001. IUCN Red List Categories and Criteria: Version 3.1. IUCN Species Survival Commission. IUCN, Gland, Switzerland, and Cambridge, UK. 30 pp.

IUCN. 2004. Guidelines for Using the IUCN Red List Categories and Criteria. IUCN Species Survival Commission. IUCN, Gland, Switzerland, and Cambridge, UK. 50 pp.

IWC. 1995. Chairman's report of the forty-sixth annual meeting. Report of the International Whaling Commission 45:1552.

Kenyon, K. W. 1969. The sea otter in the eastern Pacific Ocean. North American Fauna 68. U.S. Department of the Interior, Washington D.C.

Krahn, M. M., P. R. Wade, S. T. Kalinowski, M. E. Dahlheim, B. L. Taylor, M. B. Hanson, G. M. Ylitalo, R. P. Angliss, J. E. Stein, and R. S. Waples. 2002. Status review of Southern Resident killer whales (*Orcinus orca*) under the Endangered Species Act. NOAA Tech. Memo. NMFS-NWFSC-54. 133 pp.

Krahn, M. M., M. J. Ford, W. F. Perrin, P. R. Wade, R. P. Angliss, M. B. Hanson, B. L. Taylor, G. M. Ylitalo, M. E. Dahlheim, J. E. Stein, and R. S. Waples. 2004. Status review of Southern

Resident killer whales *(Orcinus orca)* under the Endangered Species Act. NOAA Tech. Memo. NMFS-NWFSC-62. 73 pp.

Kretzmann, M. B., N. J. Gemmell, and A. Meyer. 2001. Microsatellite analysis of population structure in the endangered Hawaiian monk seal. Conservation Biology 15:457–466.

Kretzmann, M. B., W. G. Gilmartin, A. Meyer, G. P. Zegers, S. R. Fain, B. F. Taylor, and D. P. Costa. 1997. Low genetic variability in the Hawaiian monk seal. Conservation Biology 11:482–490.

Laidre, K. L, R. J. Jameson, and D. P. DeMaster. 2001. An estimate of carrying capacity for sea otters along the California coast. Marine Mammal Science 17:294–306.

Le Boeuf, B., K. W. Kenyon, and B. Villa-Ramirez. 1986. The Caribbean monk seal is extinct. Marine Mammal Science 2:70–72.

Lefebvre, L. W., T. J. O'Shea, G. B. Rathbun, and R. C. Best. 1989. Distribution, status, and biogeography of the West Indian manatee. Biogeography of the West Indies 1989:567–610.

Lowry, L., G. O'Corry-Crowe, and D. Goodman. 2006. *Delphinapterus leucas* (Cook Inlet population). *In* IUCN 2006. 2006 IUCN Red List of Threatened Species.

NRC. 2003. The decline of the Steller sea lion in Alaskan waters: untangling food webs and fishing nets. National Academies Press, Washington, D.C. 216 pp.

NMFS. 1991a. Final Recovery Plan for the Humpback Whale *Megaptera novaeangliae*. National Marine Fisheries Service, Silver Spring, MD. 105 pp.

NMFS. 1991b. Final Recovery Plan for the Northern Right Whale *Eubalaena glacialis*. National Marine Fisheries Service, Silver Spring, MD. 86 pp.

NMFS. 1992. Final Recovery Plan for Steller Sea Lions, *Eumetopias jubatus*. National Marine Fisheries Service, Silver Spring, MD. 92 pp.

NMFS. 1993. Conservation Plan for the Northern Fur Seal, *Callorhinus ursinus*. National Marine Fisheries Service, Silver Spring, MD. 74 pp.

NMFS. 1995. Status review of the United States Steller sea lion, *Eumetopias jubatus*, population. National Marine Fisheries Service, National Marine Mammal Laboratory, Seattle, WA. 61 pp.

NMFS. 1998a. Recovery Plan for the Blue Whale, *Balaenoptera musculus*. National Marine Fisheries Service, Silver Spring, MD. 30 pp.

NMFS 1998b. Draft Recovery Plan for the Fin Whale *Balaenoptera physalus* and the Sei Whale *Balaenoptera borealis*. National Marine Fisheries Service, Silver Spring, MD. 65 pp.

NMFS. 2005. Recovery Plan for the North Atlantic Right Whale (*Eubalaena glacialis*). National Marine Fisheries Service, Silver Spring, MD. 138 pp.

NMFS. In prep.(a). Recovery Plan for the Hawaiian Monk Seal. National Marine Fisheries Service, Silver Spring, MD.

NMFS. In prep.(b). Recovery Plan for the Steller Sea Lion. National Marine Fisheries Service, Silver Spring, MD.

NMFS. In prep.(c). Conservation Plan for the Cook Inlet Beluga Whale (*Delphinapterus leucas*). National Marine Fisheries Service, Juneau, AK.

O'Corry-Crowe, G. M, R. S. Suydam, A. Rosenberg, K. J. Frost, and A. E. Dizon. 1997. Phylogeography, population structure and dispersal patterns of the beluga whale *Delphinapterus leucas* in the western Nearctic revealed by mitochondrial DNA. Molecular Ecology 6:955–970.

Perry, S. L., D. P. DeMaster, and G. K. Silber. 1999. The great whales: history and status of six species listed as endangered under the U.S. Endangered Species Act of 1973. Marine Fisheries Review 61:1–74.

Pitcher, K. W., P. F. Olesiuk, R. F. Brown, M. S. Lowry, S. J. Jeffries, J. L. Sease, W. L. Perryman, C. E. Stinchcomb, and L. F. Lowry. 2007. Abundance and distribution of the eastern North Pacific Steller sea lion (*Eumetopias jubatus*) population. Fishery Bulletin 107:102–115.

Ragen, T. J., and D. M. Lavigne. 1999. The Hawaiian Monk Seal: Biology of an Endangered Species. Pages 224–245 *in* J. R. Twiss and R. R Reeves (eds.), Conservation and Management of Marine Mammals. Smithsonian Institution Press, Washington, D.C.

Ralls, K., D. DeMaster, and J. Estes. 1996. Developing a delisting criterion for the southern sea otter under the U. S. Endangered Species Act. Conservation Biology 10:1528–1537.

Read, A. J., B. Foster, K. Urian, B. Wilson, and D. Waples. 2003. Abundance of bottlenose dolphins in the bays, sounds, and estuaries of North Carolina. Marine Mammal Science 19:59–73.

Reeves, R. R. 2001. Overview of catch history, historic abundance and distribution of right whales in the western North Atlantic and in Cintra Bay, West Africa. Journal of Cetacean Research and Management 2:187–192.

Reeves, R. R., B. D. Smith, E. A. Crespo, and G. N. di Sciara (compilers). 2003. Dolphins, Whales and Porpoises: 2002–2010 Conservation Action Plan for the World's Cetaceans. IUCN/SSC Cetacean Specialist Group. IUCN, Gland, Switzerland, and Cambridge, UK. 139 pp.

Reeves, R. R., W. F. Perrin, B. L. Taylor, C. S. Baker, and S. L. Mesnick (eds.). 2004. Report of the Workshop on Shortcomings of Cetacean Taxonomy in Relation to Needs of Conservation and Management, April 30–May 2, 2004, La Jolla, CA. 94 pp.

Reijnders, P., S. Brasseur, J. van der Toorn, P. van der Wolf, I. Boyd, J. Harwood, D. Lavigne, and L. Lowry. 1993. Seals, Fur Seals, Sea Lions, and Walrus: status survey and conservation action plan. IUCN, Gland, Switzerland. 88 pp.

Rice, D. W. 1973. Caribbean monk seal (*Monachus tropicalis*). IUCN Survival Service Commission. IUCN Pub. New Series Supplementary Paper 39:98–112.

Rice, D. W. 1998. Marine Mammals of the World: Systematics and Distribution. Society for Marine Mammalogy, Spec. Publ. No. 4. Allen Press, Lawrence, KS. 231 pp.

Rosenbaum, H. C., R. L. Brownell, W. M. Brown, et al. 2000. World-wide genetic differentiation of *Eubalaena*: questioning the number of right whale species. Molecular Ecology 9:1793–1802.

Runge, M. C., C. A. Langtimm, and W. L. Kendall. 2004. A stage-based model of manatee population dynamics. Marine Mammal Science 20:361–385.

Scott, G. P., D. M. Burn, and L. J. Hansen. 1988. The dolphin die off: long term effects and recovery of the population. Proceedings: Oceans '88, IEEE Cat. No. 88-CH2585-8, Vol.3:819–823.

Shelden, K. E. W., D. P. DeMaster, D. J. Rugh, and A. M. Olson. 2001. Developing classification criteria under the U.S. Endangered Species Act: bowhead whales as a case study. Conservation Biology 15:1300–1307.

Shelden, K. W., S. E. Moore, J. M. Waite, P. R. Wade, and D. J. Rugh. 2005. Historic and current habitat use by North Pacific right whales *Eubalaena japonica* in the Bering Sea and Gulf of Alaska. Mammal Review 35:129–155.

Shelden, K. E. W., and D. J. Rugh. 1995. The bowhead whale, *Balaena mysticetus*: its historic and current status. Marine Fisheries Review 57(3–4):1–20.

Springer, A. M., J. A. Estes, G. B. van Vliet, T. M. Williams, D. F. Doak, E. M. Danner, K. A. Forney, and B. Pfister. 2003. Sequential megafaunal collapse in the North Pacific Ocean: An ongoing legacy of industrial whaling? Proceedings of the National Academy of Sciences 100:12223–12228.

Stevick, P. T, J. Allen, P. J. Clapham, N. Friday, S. K. Katona, F. Larsen, J. Lien, D. K. Mattila, P. J. Palsbol, J. Sigurjonsson, T. D. Smith, N. Oien, and P. S. Hamilton. 2003. North Atlantic humpback whale abundance and rate of increase for decades after protection from whaling. Marine Ecology Progress Series 258:263–273.

Taylor, B. 2005. Identifying units to conserve. Pages 149–162 *in* J. E. Reynolds, W. F. Perrin, R. R. Reeves, S. Montgomery, and T. J. Ragen (eds.), Marine Mammal Research, Conservation beyond Crisis. Johns Hopkins University Press, Baltimore, MD.

Taylor, C. R., J. Reynolds, and A. Brautigam. 2006. Support of the SSG Sirenian Symposium and IUCN Red List Assessments, Ninth International Mammalogical Congress. Final Report to Conservation International Foundation. 16 pp.

Weber, M. L, and D. W. Laist. 2007. The status of protection programs for endangered, threatened, and depleted marine mammals in U.S. waters. Final report prepared for the Marine Mammal Commission, Bethesda, MD.

Wilson, D. E., M. A. Bogan, R. L. Brownell, Jr., A. M. Burdin, and M. K. Maminov. 1991. Geographic variation in sea otters, *Enhydra lutris*. Journal of Mammalogy. 72:22–36.

Woodby, D. A., and D. B. Botkin. 1993. Stock sizes prior to commercial whaling. Pages 387–407 *in* J. J. Burns, J. J. Montague, and C. J. Cowles (eds.), The Bowhead Whale. Society for Marine Mammalogy, Spec. Publ. No. 2.

Woods, C. A. 1987. An investigation of possible sightings of Caribbean monk seals (*Monachus tropicalis*) along the north coast of Haiti. Final report to the Marine Mammal Commission. National Technical Information Service, NTIS PB-285 410. Springfield, VA. 89 pp.

Table 1.   International Union for the Conservation of Nature classification categories (IUCN 2001)

EXTINCT (EX)

A taxon is Extinct when there is no reasonable doubt that the last individual has died. A taxon is presumed Extinct when exhaustive surveys in known and/or expected habitat, at appropriate times (diurnal, seasonal, annual), throughout its historic range have failed to record an individual. Surveys should be over a time frame appropriate to the taxon's life cycle and life form.

EXTINCT IN THE WILD (EW)

A taxon is Extinct in the Wild when it is known only to survive in cultivation, in captivity or as a naturalized population (or populations) well outside the past range. A taxon is presumed Extinct in the Wild when exhaustive surveys in known and/or expected habitat, at appropriate times (diurnal, seasonal, annual), throughout its historic range have failed to record an individual. Surveys should be over a time frame appropriate to the taxon's life cycle and life form.

CRITICALLY ENDANGERED (CR)

A taxon is Critically Endangered when the best available evidence indicates that it meets any of the criteria A to E for Critically Endangered, and it is therefore considered to be facing an extremely high risk of extinction in the wild.

ENDANGERED (EN)

A taxon is Endangered when the best available evidence indicates that it meets any of the criteria A to E for Endangered, and it is therefore considered to be facing a very high risk of extinction in the wild.

VULNERABLE (VU)

A taxon is Vulnerable when the best available evidence indicates that it meets any of the criteria A to E for Vulnerable, and it is therefore considered to be facing a high risk of extinction in the wild.

NEAR THREATENED (NT)

A taxon is Near Threatened when it has been evaluated against the criteria but does not qualify for Critically Endangered, Endangered or Vulnerable now but is close to qualifying for or is likely to qualify for a threatened category in the near future.

LEAST CONCERN (LC)

A taxon is Least Concern when it has been evaluated against the criteria and does not qualify for Critically Endangered, Endangered, Vulnerable or Near Threatened. Widespread and abundant taxa are included in this category.

DATA DEFICIENT (DD)

A taxon is Data Deficient when there is inadequate information to make a direct, or indirect, assessment of its risk of extinction based on its distribution and/or population status. A taxon in this category may be well studied, and its biology well known, but appropriate data on abundance and/or distribution are lacking. Data Deficient is therefore not a category of threat. Listing of taxa in this category indicates that more information is required and acknowledges the possibility that future research will show that threatened classification is appropriate. It is important to make positive use of whatever data are available. In many cases great care should be exercised in choosing between Data Deficient and a threatened status. If the range of a taxon is suspected to be relatively circumscribed, if a considerable period of time has elapsed since the last record of the taxon, threatened status may well be justified.

Table 2. Marine mammal taxa currently listed as endangered or threatened under the ESA or depleted under the MMPA, with the current IUCN classification also shown

Taxon name	ESA listing	IUCN classification	MMPA listing
West Indian manatee, Florida population	Endangered	Vulnerable	Depleted
West Indian manatee, Antillean population	Endangered	Vulnerable	Depleted
Southern sea otter	Threatened	Endangered[11]	Depleted
Northern sea otter, southwest AK population	Threatened	Endangered[11]	Depleted
Caribbean monk seal	Endangered	Extinct	Depleted
Hawaiian monk seal	Endangered	Endangered	Depleted
Guadalupe fur seal	Threatened	Vulnerable	Depleted
Northern fur seal, eastern Pacific population	Not listed	Vulnerable[11]	Depleted
Steller sea lion, eastern population	Threatened	Endangered[11]	Depleted
Steller sea lion, western population	Endangered	Endangered[11]	Depleted
Blue whale	Endangered	Endangered[12]	Depleted
Bowhead whale, western Arctic population	Endangered	Lower risk, cd[13]	Depleted
Fin whale	Endangered	Endangered[11]	Depleted
Humpback whale	Endangered	Vulnerable[11]	Depleted
North Atlantic right whale	Endangered	Endangered	Depleted
North Pacific right whale	Endangered	Endangered	Depleted
Sei whale	Endangered	Endangered[11]	Depleted
Sperm whale	Endangered	Vulnerable	Depleted
Beluga whale, Cook Inlet population	Not listed	Critically endangered	Depleted
Bottlenose dolphin, mid-Atlantic coastal population	Not listed	Data deficient[11]	Depleted
Killer whale, southern resident population	Endangered	Lower risk, cd[11,13]	Depleted
Killer whale, AT1 group	Not listed	Lower risk, cd[11,13]	Depleted

---

[11] Listing applies to the entire species worldwide; individual populations have not been evaluated.

[12] Listing applies to the entire species worldwide; North Pacific population listed as lower risk; North Atlantic population as vulnerable.

[13] See note 3 above.

Table 3. Conservation units used to evaluate status of selected large whale species in the ESA, IUCN, and MMPA evaluation systems

Species name	Currently accepted taxonomy	ESA listing	IUCN evaluation	MMPA Stock assessment reports
Blue whale	Single species with one Northern Hemisphere subspecies	Entire species	Worldwide	Western North Atlantic Eastern North Pacific Western North Pacific
Fin whale	Single species with one Northern Hemisphere subspecies	Entire species	Worldwide	Western North Atlantic California-Oregon-Washington Northeastern Pacific Hawaii
Humpback whale	Single species with no recognized subspecies	Entire species[14]	Worldwide	Gulf of Maine Eastern North Pacific Central North Pacific Western North Pacific
Sei whale	Single species with one Northern Hemisphere subspecies	Entire species	Worldwide	Nova Scotia Eastern North Pacific Hawaii
Sperm whale	Single species with no recognized subspecies	Entire species	Worldwide	North Atlantic California-Oregon-Washington North Pacific Hawaii Gulf of Mexico

---

[14] The recovery plan for humpback whales recognizes three populations in the western North Atlantic, central North Pacific, and eastern North Pacific.

Table 4. Summary of the biological status of marine mammal taxa currently listed as endangered or threatened under the ESA or depleted under the MMPA

Taxon	Current population size	Current population trend	Population size relative to historical level
Endangered Species			
West Indian manatee, Florida	>3,300	Increasing?	Unknown
West Indian manatee, Antillean	Unknown	Declining?	Reduced?
Caribbean monk seal	0	N/A	Extinct
Hawaiian monk seal	1,252	Declining 1.9 percent per year	Reduced 60 percent from 1958
Steller sea lion, western population	38,513	Increasing?	Reduced 81 percent from 1970s
Blue whale[15]	>2,994	Increasing?	Reduced
Bowhead whale, western Arctic population	10,545	Increasing 3.4 percent per year	Reduced 54 percent from the 1800s
Fin whale	>11,970	Unknown	Reduced
Humpback whale	>6,692	Increasing	Reduced
North Atlantic right whale	299	Declining?	Reduced
North Pacific right whale, eastern population	>23	Unknown	Reduced
Sei whale[16]	>133	Unknown	Reduced
Sperm whale[17]	>14,468	Unknown	Reduced
Killer whale, southern resident population	84	Unknown	Reduced 40 percent from historical levels
Threatened Species			
Southern sea otter	2,825	Increasing?	Reduced
Northern sea otter, southwest Alaska population	41,865	Declining	Reduced 55 to 67 percent from 1976
Guadalupe fur seal	7,408	Increasing	Reduced
Steller sea lion, eastern population	44,996	Increasing	Unknown

---

[15] Data not available for the North Atlantic and western North Pacific stocks.
[16] Data not available for the Nova Scotia stock.
[17] Data not available for the North Pacific stock.

Table 4. Summary of the biological status of marine mammal taxa currently listed as
endangered or threatened under the ESA or depleted under the MMPA
(continued)

Taxon	Current population size	Current population trend	Population size relative to historical level
Species Listed Only as Depleted			
Northern fur seal, eastern population	688,028	Declining	Reduced 65 percent from the 1950s
Beluga whale, Cook Inlet population	278	Declining?	Reduced 57 percent from 1994
Bottlenose dolphin, mid-Atlantic coastal population	33,000	Unknown	Reduced
Killer whale, AT1 group	8	Declining	Reduced 64 percent from 1988

Table 5. Summary of the quality of available data for marine mammal taxa currently listed as endangered or threatened under the ESA or depleted under the MMPA (G=good, F=fair, P=poor)

Taxon name	Total population size	Trend in pop. size	Popula-tion structure	Vital rates	Habitat needs	Limiting factors
West Indian manatee, Florida	G	G	G	G	G	G
West Indian manatee, Antillean	P	P	P	P	F	F
Southern sea otter	G	G	G	G	G	F
Northern sea otter, southwest Alaska	G	G	F	F	G	F
Caribbean monk seal	—	—	—	—	—	—
Hawaiian monk seal	G	G	G	G	G	G
Guadalupe fur seal	P	P	P	P	P	P
Northern fur seal, eastern Pacific	G	G	G	F	F	F
Steller sea lion, eastern population	G	G	G	F	F	F
Steller sea lion, western population	G	G	G	F	F	F
Blue whale	P	P	P	P	P	P
Bowhead whale, western Arctic	G	G	F	F	F	F
Fin whale	F	P	P	F	P	P
Humpback whale[18]	F	F	F	F	F	F
North Atlantic right whale	F	F	G	G	F	G
North Pacific right whale	P	P	P	P	P	P
Sei whale	P	P	P	P	P	P
Sperm whale	F	P	F	F	P	P
Beluga whale, Cook Inlet	G	G	G	P	F	F
Bottlenose dolphin, mid-Atlantic coastal	P	P	P	P	F	F
Killer whale, southern resident	G	G	G	G	F	F
Killer whale, AT1 group	G	G	G	G	F	P

---

[18] Results from the SPLASH project should greatly improve data available for North Pacific populations.

Table 6. ESA and MMPA listings of taxa with good or fair data in at least five data categories (grouped by listing status and arranged within groups in order of increasing abundance)

Taxon name	Current pop. size	Current pop. trend	Relative pop. size	ESA/MMPA listing
Killer whale, southern resident	84	Unknown	Reduced 41 percent	Endangered
North Atlantic right whale	299	Declining?	Reduced	Endangered
Hawaiian monk seal	1,252	Declining	Reduced 60 percent	Endangered
West Indian manatee, Florida	>3,300	Increasing?	Unknown	Endangered
Humpback whale	>6,692	Increasing	Reduced	Endangered
Bowhead whale, western Arctic	10,545	Increasing	Reduced 57 percent	Endangered
Steller sea lion, western population	38,513	Increasing?	Reduced 82 percent	Endangered
Southern sea otter	2,825	Increasing?	Reduced	Threatened
Steller sea lion, eastern population	44,996	Increasing	Unknown	Threatened
Northern sea otter, southwest Alaska	41,865	Declining	Reduced 62 percent	Threatened
Killer whale, AT1 group	8	Declining	Reduced 59 percent	Depleted
Beluga whale, Cook Inlet	278	Declining?	Reduced 72 percent	Depleted
Northern fur seal, eastern Pacific	688,028	Declining	Reduced 60 percent	Depleted

VII. APPENDIX

Summary of Quantitative Features of the IUCN Rule-based Approach

See IUCN (2001) for a more complete description of the criteria. Bolding indicates the differences between the classifications of "critically endangered," "endangered," and "vulnerable." (wl) = "whichever is longer, up to a maximum of 100 years." (From DeMaster et al. 2004)

Critically endangered

A.   Reduction in population size
- $\geq$ **90 percent** decline in past **10** years or **3** generations (wl), if understood and reversible and stopped
- $\geq$ **80 percent** decline in past **10** years or **3** generations (wl), if not understood or reversible or stopped
- $\geq$ **80 percent** decline projected for next **10** years or **3** generations (wl)
- $\geq$ **80 percent** decline including past and future **10** years or **3** generations (wl), if not understood or reversible or stopped

B.   Geographic range
- extent of occurrence < **100** km^2
- area of occupancy < **10** km^2

C.   Population size < **250** mature individuals and:
- continuing decline $\geq$ **25 percent** in future **3** years or **1** generation (wl)
- no subpopulation with > **50** mature individuals, or $\geq$ **90 percent** mature individuals in one subpopulation

D.   Population size < **50** mature individuals

E.   Quantitative analysis showing Pr(extinction) $\geq$ **50 percent** within **10** years or **3** generations (wl)

Endangered

A.   Reduction in population size
- $\geq$ **70 percent** decline in past **10** years or **3** generations (wl), if understood and reversible and stopped
- $\geq$ **50 percent** decline in past **10** years or **3** generations (wl), if not understood or reversible or stopped
- $\geq$ **50 percent** decline projected for next **10** years or **3** generations (wl)
- $\geq$ **50 percent** decline including past and future **10** years or **3** generations (wl), if not understood or reversible or stopped

B.   Geographic range
- extent of occurrence < **5000** km^2
- area of occupancy < **500** km^2

C.   Population size < **2,500** mature individuals and:
- continuing decline $\geq$ **20 percent** in future **5** years or **2** generations (wl)

• no subpopulation with > **250** mature individuals, or ≥ **95 percent** mature individuals in one subpopulation
D. Population size < **250** mature individuals
E. Quantitative analysis showing Pr(extinction) ≥ **20 percent** within **20** years or **5** generations (wl)

Vulnerable

A. Reduction in population size
   • ≥ **50 percent** decline in past **10** years or **3** generations (wl), if understood and reversible and stopped
   • ≥ **30 percent** decline in past **10** years or **3** generations (wl), if not understood or reversible or stopped
   • ≥ **30 percent** decline projected for next **10** years or **3** generations (wl)
   • ≥ **30 percent** decline including past and future **10** years or **3** generations (wl), if not understood or reversible or stopped
B. Geographic range
   • extent of occurrence < **20,000** km^2
   • area of occupancy < **2000** km^2
C. Population size < **10,000** mature individuals and:
   • continuing decline ≥ **25 percent** in future **10** years or **3** generations (wl)
   • no subpopulation with > **1,000** mature individuals, or **100 percent** mature individuals in one
   subpopulation
D. Population size < **1,000** mature individuals
E. Quantitative analysis showing Pr(extinction) ≥ **10 percent** within **100** years (wl)